It's Not
Mean
If It's
True

It's Not Mean If It's True

MORE TRIALS FROM MY QUEER LIFE

MICHAEL THOMAS FORD

alyson books
los angeles | new york

MANUFACTURED IN THE UNITED STATES OF AMERICA.

THIS TRADE PAPERBACK ORIGINAL IS PUBLISHED BY
ALYSON PUBLICATIONS,
P.O. BOX 4371, LOS ANGELES, CA 90078-4371.
DISTRIBUTION IN THE UNITED KINGDOM BY
TURNAROUND PUBLISHER SERVICES LTD.,
UNIT 3, OLYMPIA TRADING ESTATE,
COBURG ROAD, WOOD GREEN,
LONDON N22 6TZ ENGLAND.

FIRST EDITION: SEPTEMBER 2000

00 01 02 03 04 **a** 10 9 8 7 6 5 4 3 2 1

ISBN 1-55583-599-6

LIBRARY OF CONGRESS CATALOGING-IN-PUBLICATION
    FORD, MICHAEL THOMAS.
      IT'S NOT MEAN IF IT'S TRUE : MORE TRIALS FROM MY
    QUEER LIFE / MICHAEL THOMAS FORD.
        ISBN 1-55583-599-6
        1. HOMOSEXUALITY—HUMOR. 2. GAY MEN—HUMOR.
    3. GAY WIT AND HUMOR. I. TITLE.
    PN6231.H57 F675 2000
    814'.54—DC21   00-032768

CREDITS
COVER PHOTOGRAPHY AND DESIGN BY B. ZINDA.

For Roger McElhiney,
who stops me from making big mistakes and then
gets me to make even bigger ones.

Contents

Author's Note ii

Fame 1
Prom Queen 8
I Want *My* MTV 14
The Condensed History of Gay Pride 20
Gym Dandy 25
Odd Ducks 31
Size Matters 35
Getting Personal: A Beginner's Guide to
    Advertising for Love .40
Runaway Train 48
Not What the Doctor Ordered 53
Playing It Straight 60
It Is Hereby Resolved 66
Rite of Passage 72
Cheaper by the Dozen 78
The Nicks Fix 84
Welcome to the Real World 90
Sticker Shock 97
When You Wish Upon a Star 103
Growing Pains 109
The Condensed Guide to First Dates 115
High Times 120
Test of Faith 126
It's Not Mean If It's True 133
The Condensed History of Queer Cinema 140

Viagra Falls 145
Overeducated Consumer 151
Endangered Species 157
Ah-Choo!: A Guide to the New
    Hankie Code 163
Out of Style 169
What a Concept 175
Green-Eyed Monster 179
Thou Shalt Not Have Any Common Sense . . .185
Et Tu, Po? 192
It's All in the Cards 199
Do You Have Any That Are Already Trained? . . .204
The Condensed History of Queer Sex 210
Along Came a Spider 215
If the Shoe Fits 219
Why I Am Queer 225

About the Author 231

Author's Note

As I prepare to send this third collection of essays to my editor, I'm amazed at the number of people I have to thank. I thought for sure I must have mentioned everyone I know the first two times around, but now I find myself with a new list of people whose help and support have been invaluable to me over the past year. Fortunately, this just means that a lot more people have come into my life as a result of the first two books. That's one of the unexpected gifts you receive as a writer: Readers discover your work and let you know how it has affected them. Sometimes this connection is as brief as a single letter or an exchange of E-mail. Other times new friendships are born. My life is richer now because of the people who took time to share their stories with me.

So, in addition to the usual cast of characters who make my life more interesting (and you all know who you are because your names were in the other books), I owe many thanks to the following friends—old and new—for their advice, laughter, and hand-holding: Juliet Swiggum, Dave Morgan, Sarah Higdon, Dominic Sheehan, Mike Mehring, Ken Platek, Merrilee Heifetz, Dan Cullinane, Charlie Keating, Angela Brown, Warren Dunford,

Gabriel Goldberg, Eve Becker, Al Whitehurst, Rick Andreoli, Scott Sophos, Michael Elliott, Scarlett Fever, Robrt Pela, Dave Hooban, Gretchen Breese, Jay Kawarsky, Drew Poling, Scott Brassart, Robert Hines, Hollis Lilly, Shelley Bindon, and all my friends from the Jamaica Pond Dog Group. Thank you too to all of you who read the other books and told your friends to pick them up. I appreciate it more than you know, and I hope you're just as pleased this time around.

Oh, and before you dive in and start enjoying yourselves, there's one little editorial note I feel compelled to make: Somewhere between the writing of the earliest pieces in this book and the last ones, I fell in love. This is great, but it wreaks havoc with certain editorial themes, particularly in the earlier essays. There are things I wrote B.D. (Before Dave) that don't apply A.D. (After Dave). For a variety of reasons—most of them geographic and none of them tragic—Dave and I are no longer together. But he was an integral part of my life for a year (and still is), and he appears in a number of pieces in this collection. I figured I'd better mention this right up front. I know how you all get when you don't know exactly what's going on.

There. Now you're up to speed. I think it's safe to proceed. Just remember that we're all friends here. If I say anything that you don't like, keep in mind that I never mentioned it when you forgot my birthday.

Fame

I ought to be famous. I say this because my name has appeared in an issue of *Entertainment Weekly*. Harrison Ford is on the cover, and I am on page 118. I have the clipping to prove it.

Never mind that not one of my many friends who eagerly devour the magazine each week even noticed my mention, and that I only found out about it when one of the guys at the gym said, "Someone with the same name as yours is in the new *Entertainment Weekly*. Isn't that weird?" Forget for a moment that there is only one sentence about me. Ignore the fact that the only reason I'm there at all is because I put Alec Baldwin's name in the title of one of my books and someone thought it would be amusing to point this out. These things are not important. What's important is that I am in *Entertainment Weekly*, right there in the same paragraph with Al Franken. I think that entitles me to something.

I have always loved those stories in which some small incident starts a chain of events that results in fantastic good luck for someone. You know, like when you hear an actor talking about how only six months ago he was living in squalor and licking the stains on the couch because he couldn't afford food, but then some director happened to catch a commercial he made for shaving cream and decided to cast him in the biggest movie of the summer, launching him into superstardom. Or when some television mogul on a cross-country flight needs something to pass the time and reads a really great book by this writer he's never heard of but whose book he picked up because it was the first thing he saw at the newsstand, then likes it so much he calls the writer to see if maybe he'd like to try writing a sitcom, ending that writer's worries about paying rent.

These are very nice stories. Unfortunately, they do not happen nearly as often as one would like, especially if you are one of the struggling actors or writers waiting for one of these life-changing phone calls. It is all well and good to believe that just when you are on the brink of running out of money and becoming homeless that the manuscript you sent out a year ago and forgot about will be bought for a million dollars by someone who has just plucked it from the pile on his desk. In my experience, however, what is more likely to happen is that while you're waiting for the phone call that will change your life, your agent will send you an E-mail informing you that she has just returned from a meeting at which it was decided that no one likes you and you should die.

Still, I try to remain optimistic. So when I discovered my name in *Entertainment Weekly* I was fully prepared for the phone to start ringing off the hook with offers from people in Hollywood. I didn't know what kind of offers exactly, but I had ideas. I thought surely they would find the title of my book so hysterical that they would beg me to turn my talents to the screen, big or small; I didn't care which one. After all, I'd always been told that agents and executives scan the pages of such magazines looking for previously unknown talent to exploit. Surely at least one would see my mention and decide he had to have me.

Well, this did not happen. During the first couple of days after the issue hit the stands, I barely left the house. I knew that if I did I would miss a call from Steven Spielberg or the producers of *Will & Grace* begging me to lend my talents to their latest endeavors. I blamed their silence on the fact that I was on page 118 and they probably hadn't gotten that far yet, being busy with other matters like deciding where to take me to lunch once they found me. I fantasized about what I would do with all the money they were certain to offer (get the dog a new hip and me a haircut), and I checked the phone often to make sure it was working properly.

When the next week rolled around and the Harrison Ford issue was replaced with the Jennifer Lopez issue, I started to worry. Everyone knows that last week's news is ancient history in Tinseltown, and now I was competing with a whole new crop of would-be stars. I opened the magazine and flipped through it anxiously to see what I was up against. Then I saw it. There on page 34, a whole 84 pages before my mention had appeared, I found an article about some 19-year-old college student who had been paid nearly a million dollars for his first novel, which some studio exec on a cross-country flight happened to read and decide to make into a movie for that oh-so-desirable 18- to 24-year-old market.

I handled this as well as could be expected. I took out the clipping with my name in it and stared at it while stifling the racking sobs that longed to break forth from my throat. Maybe, I tried to convince myself, it was enough just to be mentioned. Isn't that what the people who lose at the Oscars always say while they smile and reach for the Prozac in their handbags? But in my heart I knew it wasn't. I'd gotten so close. I was in the same issue with Harrison Ford. But it was the wrong Ford on the cover. I wanted it to be me up front and him on page 118.

Maybe I wouldn't want fame so badly if I hadn't already had a little taste of it. A few years ago I wrote a number of young adult novels based on a sort of successful television series. There happen to be quite a lot of children on my block, and some of them read these books and realized I was the person who wrote them. From that moment on I became The Writer Guy. Every time I took my dog, Roger, for a walk, a little group of 10-year-olds would cluster around and ask if they could pet him. Afterward, they'd run off looking at their hands as if they'd never wash them again. Sometimes they would drag their little friends home with them and point me out when I walked past. "There goes The Writer Guy," they'd say, and their friends would stare at me with the same awe they reserved for the Backstreet Boys. I found out later that one enterprising little girl was giving her schoolmates tours of my front porch for a quarter a head.

I know, groupies who don't come up to your waist and have no disposable income are hardly something to get excited about. But it was fun being The Writer Guy for a while, at least until the kids started asking why my books weren't as popular as the Goosebumps and Animorphs series, at which point I started walking the dog on a different route.

And at least the kids were excited about seeing a real live writer. Adults couldn't care less. Only twice have I ever been recognized in public because of my books for adults or from my newspaper columns. Once was at a bookstore, where a man charged over to me and said, "I know you. You're that guy who signed my book." It took a minute for him to remember *which* guy and *which* book, but eventually he did, at which point he smiled and said, "You have a nice signature." Just what every writer in search of fame wants to hear.

The second time my writing brought me a fleeting moment of celebrity was at the gym, where I was standing in the locker room after having just run five miles on the treadmill. I was contemplating the thrill of a post-workout shower when I had the strange sensation that someone behind me was staring at me—very hard. I turned around and discovered a man gazing with great concentration at my butt.

"You're the guy who wrote that column about your ass, aren't you?" he said.

I had, in fact, recently written a newspaper column about this very subject. However, this is a very disconcerting question to be asked when one is standing, holding nothing but a sweaty jockstrap, in front of a stranger. All I could do was nod.

"I thought I recognized you," he said, and walked out without saying another word.

You'd think I would be excited over finally being noticed. But having someone recognize me because of my ass was not really what I had in mind when I dreamed about fame. Besides, now I was convinced that every single man in my gym was secretly looking at my butt and forming opinions about it. Probably they all talked about it when I wasn't there and smiled meaningfully at one another when I passed by. This was not reassuring in the least.

I suppose it's better than what I usually get, though. Many times I've walked into bookstores where I'm scheduled to do a reading, only to have the salespeople look at me blankly when I walk up to the counter. "You don't look like you," is the usual response when I finally tell them who I am. I'm not sure what this means, but it unnerves me, like I'm running around impersonating myself and pretty soon someone is going to get me for it.

My friends think this is funny. Once, while standing in line at a local gay bookstore to pay for our purchases, my friend Mark David noticed that my book *That's Mr. Faggot to You* was right next to the cash register with a big #1 BEST-SELLER sign on it. When he reached the counter, he picked up a copy of the book—which has my picture right on the front cover—and turned to the very bored-looking clerk. "Is this any good?" he asked.

The young man looked at the book, looked right at me, and said, "Everyone seems to love it, but I don't see what the big deal is. I didn't think it was that good."

Luckily for everyone involved, I was too tired to be horrified. Instead, when it was my turn to pay, I handed the clerk my credit card. He looked at the name on it, then looked at me, then looked at my picture on the cover of the book. He turned an interesting shade of red and said, "Oh, these are on the house, Mr. Ford." I left wishing I'd bought more. But it's always nice to get porn magazines for free, so I'm not complaining.

I guess the whole fame thing is relative. Several times

reporters and readers have said to me, "It must be so nice to be at the height of your career." I'm sure these people all have the best of intentions, but I can't help wondering what they think my life is like. To me, fame means not having to clean my own house and not worrying about things like buying food and paying rent. That and being best friends with Cher.

But I have none of these things. Instead I'm still walking around picking up the dog's poop myself and wondering if anyone will buy one of my kidneys for a lot of money. And the only way I'll ever get to see Cher is if I pay for it. Even then I can only afford the cheap seats, so all I'll really get to see is a kind of blurry miniature Cher waving from a distant stage. But at least everyone in the stadium would know that it was Cher. What's even sadder is that while one person recognized my ass, millions recognize hers. Even her butt is more famous than I am.

I do have friends who are truly famous, people who seldom, if ever, leave their houses because they can't go anywhere without being noticed and asked for autographs. They complain a lot about how annoying this is. Oh, boo-hoo. I feel so bad for them. It must be just awful to have people paying you gobs of money for your work because they think you're fabulous. I stay in the house most of the time too, but it's because I'm still waiting for the phone to ring.

Prom Queen

Spring is traditionally the time for high schools across the country to hold that most agonizing of teenage experiences—the senior prom. As planning committees perfect the art of making tissue paper roses and fight over choosing "Moments to Remember" or "An End and a Beginning" as the theme, girls spend the weeks preceding the event fretting about what to wear and boys spend it wondering if they'll get lucky.

For some kids, proms are wonderful events. These are generally the kids who will later look back on being head cheerleader or captain of the soccer team as the pinnacle of their lives. For the rest of high school society, the prom is a time of great worry. What kind of dress one has or whether or not dancing is something one does well can seem like the most pressing issues in the world. These are the people who will later be relieved to have only retirement accounts and mortgages to worry about. In short, most of us.

This year, things were a little more agonizing than usual for 18-year-old Charles Rice, a senior at Taylor High School in Pierson, Florida. Charles, who is gay, not only had to worry about what to wear—he had to be concerned about dancing in heels. Putting a new twist on an old theme, Charles attended his prom in full drag, sporting a stunning red satin evening gown and rhinestone accessories.

Not surprisingly, this did not go unnoticed. When Charles's plans were first revealed, school officials told him he would be barred from the event "for his own protection," even though he had previously appeared in drag at several school functions with no negative results. They reversed their decision when Rice threatened legal action, although the school's principal says no boy will be allowed to do it again in the future.

As so often is the case with such things, authority figures had the hardest time with the situation. While a handful of students grumbled that having a drag queen at their prom would spoil the fun, a more typical response came from senior Jennifer Strickland, who praised Rice's cross-dressing abilities by saying, "I've seen him dressed up and you can't tell [he's a guy] until you look at his feet." Despite rudely pointing out the age-old drag queen shame of shoe size, Jennifer's sentiments were heartfelt.

When I read about Charles, I found myself thinking back to my own high school days, when Carla Becker wore a tuxedo to the prom and everyone thought it was *soooo* cool. Carla, who played left field on the softball team and sported the prototypical dyke haircut—long in back and short all around—brought as her date a femme who wore the traditional gaudy dress with too many bows and too-big hair. The two of them danced the night away to the sounds of "I've Had the Time of My Life" while everyone applauded their individuality. It never occurred to anyone that they might be more than gal pals poking fun at prom culture.

I didn't get to see Carla and her date in person. Being the school fag, I didn't find things like dances to be wonderful opportunities for social interaction. Even though some of my female friends begged me to go with them to save them from less appealing options, I decided to stay home and think about how much above it all I was. But I heard about it in agonizing detail afterward in a long, breathless phone call from my friend Rebecca, who recounted what everyone was wearing and just how slutty Mary Lou Ackerby looked after she gave John Kernans head in the parking lot and came back with her lipstick smeared and an oil stain on her dress.

I did get a chance to experience a prom first hand, but it wasn't until my sophomore year in college, when my friend Leslie invited me to be her date to the spring formal. This was a big deal at our little religious college. It was held on a boat that sailed around New York, and it featured music, if not dancing and alcohol, both of which were forbidden. To make it even more festive, Leslie and I double-dated with my friend James and a young woman named Vickie. For various reasons, none of us had attended our high school formals, and we thought it might be fun to go together now that we were away from the hideous pressures of teen life.

Now, James and I assumed that Leslie and Vickie knew we were both gay. After all, we'd hung around with them for two years, and even though the word had never been uttered aloud (Christian colleges being the originators of the "don't ask, don't tell" policy), we thought the situation was fairly clear. In our minds, the evening was simply four friends hanging out together and having a good time, enjoying the fuss we'd skipped in high school.

James and I were wrong. As it turned out, Leslie and Vickie thought we were on dates. *Real* dates. Complete with hand-holding, flirting, and things to tell their roommates and mothers about later. This realization hit us when at one point in the evening James grabbed Vickie's stunning beaded bag and started doing his best Marilyn Monroe impression. When I joined in on the chorus of "Diamonds Are a Girl's Best Friend," the confused expressions on the girls' faces caused me to declare an emergency planning session with James in the men's room.

"What do you mean they don't know?" he said, shocked, when I voiced my suspicions. "How could they *not* know? I mean, I complimented Leslie on her *shoes*, for heaven's sake. How many straight guys would do that?"

He was right, of course, but somehow Vickie and Leslie hadn't gotten the message. Maybe they were so determined to have the prom they never had in high school that they willingly ignored the obvious. Maybe they thought that once we saw them in their fabulous dresses we'd see the light, or at least the cleavage, and come to our senses. Whatever the case, there really wasn't anything we could do about the situation except see it through. After staying in the bathroom as long as we could, we went back to the table and tried to continue as if nothing were out of the ordinary.

Except that something was out of the ordinary, and we all felt it. Now that I knew Leslie thought we were on an actual date, it was high school all over again. I didn't belong on that boat, and I didn't want to be there. To make things even worse, Mike Devin, the man I had a heartbreaking crush on, was there with his girlfriend, looking handsome as could be in his tux. As Leslie took little disinterested bites of poached fish and James tried to change the mood by pointing out landmarks of the New York skyline, I imagined dancing with the object of my obsession and feeling his big hands on my back. I felt bad for Leslie, and even worse for myself.

The rest of the event is a blur of strained conversation, nervous laughter, and an awkward ride home. Back at the dorms, as I said good night to Leslie, I fumbled with my words while she looked at her feet. Then, perhaps in a last-ditch effort to salvage her vision of what the night should have been, she kissed me. It was a restrained effort, wanting to be something more than it could be, and when it was over we quickly went our separate ways. None of us ever mentioned the night again.

I remember, several years before my own disastrous formal experience, reading Aaron Fricke's *Reflections of a Rock Lobster*, in which he writes about his battle to take a male date to his high school prom. At the time, only recently escaped from high school myself, I wondered why he would ever want to go in the first place. Now I understand. I might never have had my prom fantasy of dancing with Mike Devin come true, but I love thinking of Charles Rice dancing the night away, the lights flashing off his rhinestones as he laughs and enjoys himself with his friends. I'm proud of him—and of all the openly gay young people out there—for being who they are.

And I hope that at the end of the night Charles Rice got kissed by the man of his dreams.

I Want *My* MTV

I was one of those kids raised on MTV. I was there the day it started broadcasting, and in many ways it was my window on the world of pop culture. As a gay kid living in the middle of nowhere, it offered me a chance to see that the rest of the world wasn't the narrowly defined place my heavy-metal–loving schoolmates would have had me believe. It's where I first saw Annie Lennox and realized that people didn't have to be one thing or another. And I still vividly remember the first time I saw Boy George prance across the screen. "Hey, that girl is kind of pretty," my father said, and in my heart I knew that George and I shared the same secret from my oblivious dad.

OK, it was the early '80s. Mistakes were made. The hair was severe and the music sometimes sounded like somebody had recorded their washing machine's rinse cycle and laid some vocals over it. I never claimed that Scandal Featuring Patty Smyth was brilliant. But I did play "The Warrior" and do the hand motions when Patty sang "Shooting at the walls of heartache—bang, bang." And yes, I fell for some things I shouldn't have. Purple hair spray. Don't make me say it again.

For a while in my 20s I looked back on my MTV days with disdain. I was embarrassed by the likes of Duran Duran and Poison. They were relics from childhood, and I was quick to discard them, even disown them. It was time for more mature fare. But then Bill Clinton trotted out Fleetwood Mac to sing "Don't Stop" at his inauguration. It was touted as a reunion. *Reunion?* I thought. *That's not possible. I just saw them in concert.* But when I thought about it, I realized it had been a good five years since I'd been at that concert, and even then they were at the tail end of their heyday.

Things went from bad to worse. Suddenly we were inundated with "nostalgia" concert tours featuring the wizened likes of Pat Benatar, the Human League, and Missing Persons, bands whose records were the hottest things only yesterday. But apparently yesterday was longer ago than I remembered. Watching the rock icons of my faded youth being interviewed, I stared in horror at their paunchy faces and lined eyes and thought, *So that's what all that pancake makeup was covering up.* The guys in KISS apparently realized the same thing, because they slapped the white face back on before they hit the comeback trail.

What makes all of this even harder to take is that so many of today's youngsters are ripping off the old timers. With nothing new to say, songwriters are simply lifting the better lyrics of their predecessors, rearranging them a little, and coming up with monster hits. When The Fugees tore up the charts with their remake of "Killing Me Softly," critics oohed and aahed all over themselves at the originality. The kids who made their album a multi-platinum seller thought they'd discovered something totally new, while those of us who still have our Roberta Flack albums listened to the real thing and shook our heads sadly. More recently, I had a very heated argument with a 13-year-old who refused to believe that Janet Jackson did not write the lyrics to Joni Mitchell's "Big Yellow Taxi," which Janet sampled extensively in her hit "Got 'Til It's Gone." When I finally proved it to her by playing Joni's version, all she had to say for herself was, "How come I never saw the video for this?"

For most people, attending their first live concert is an experience firmly etched in memory. While some recall the first time they saw the Beatles, those of us from the original MTV generation had more eccentric fare. The first live concert I ever attended was the Go-Go's. A then-unknown group called INXS opened for them, and the most memorable thing about the entire show was that the big neon Go-Go's sign behind drummer Gina Schock had an O that wouldn't light, resulting in a continuously flashing "GOG-S" logo.

Once I started, I was hooked on concerts. Even if the music wasn't always great, a concert provided two or three hours of escape from the most boring place on earth for a kid with ideas. I saved the ticket stubs, and flipping through them is like reading a who's who of popular music: The Thompson Twins, Stevie Nicks, Heart, the Psychedelic Furs, Berlin, Robert Plant, the Motels, Starship, and even the Blow Monkeys. I saw them all, even if I sometimes can't remember who the hell they were.

But none of them compared to Wendy and Lisa. You remember Wendy and Lisa. They were the ultracool women who played guitar and keyboards, respectively, for Prince in his *Purple Rain* heyday. At 13, I had a huge crush on them. I thought they were the most amazing thing I'd ever seen, and I lived for Prince videos because I knew I'd get a glimpse of the two of them. Lisa was so dreamy-eyed as she stood behind her synthesizers, and Wendy rocked her way through songs like "Let's Go Crazy" and "I Would Die 4 U" as if she owned them.

Plus, I just knew they were playing on my team, even though no one talked about it. I used to play the opening to "Computer Blue," in which Wendy and Lisa have a very erotically charged exchange of dialogue, over and over. Yes, I knew they were dykes. That's why I loved them even more. In a world of gender-bending stars who all claimed to still be straight, their understated sexuality said more than George Michael's oversize CHOOSE LIFE T-shirts ever could.

When the Purple Rain tour came to a city near me, I leapt at the chance to go. I didn't care so much about Prince, but I would have given just about anything to see Wendy and Lisa. And I almost had to. My fundamentalist Christian mother swore that no child of hers would ever go to a Prince concert. But eventually I wore her down, and off I went.

It was a religious experience. While everyone else screamed for Prince and fainted at his slightest gyration, I kept my eyes firmly on Wendy and Lisa. I picked their voices out of the mix and listened for every solo Wendy had. When they did "Computer Blue," I almost threw my panties onstage.

As often happens with adolescent crushes, I forgot about Wendy and Lisa as the years passed and the music of the '80s disappeared. Then, a couple of years ago, I was talking to my friend Hillary, who lives in Los Angeles and knows lots of fabulous people.

"I have to go," she said. "We're having dinner with Wendy and Lisa."

Something in my head clicked. "You mean *the* Wendy and Lisa?" I asked. "As in the ones from the Revolution?"

"Yeah," said Hillary, clearly not understanding the importance of this moment. "We've known them for years."

To make a long story short, the next time I went to LA I insisted that Hillary arrange a dinner at which Wendy and Lisa would be present. It happened in a small, funky, macrobiotic restaurant.

I am generally not one to be impressed by other people. But I admit that this time I was nervous. This was Wendy and Lisa. I'd seen them on MTV a million times. I could close my eyes and see Wendy in her weird outfit from the "Raspberry Beret" video, looking for all the world like Clara Bow. I remembered just how Lisa's lip gloss had caught the lights in the "1999" clip. The two of them reminded me of everything that was cool about being 16 years old.

Then the door opened, and in they came. But gone were the sequins and velvets, the mile-high hair and black eyeliner. In their place were two ordinary-looking women dressed in jeans and sweatshirts. For a moment I was confused. I'd spent so long thinking of them in a certain way—as Wendy and Lisa—that I didn't recognize the people standing beside the table. Then they sat down and Hillary introduced us. All I could do was stare stupidly.

"I love you," I said finally. I'd been waiting to say it for a decade.

Wendy looked at me and laughed. Lisa took my hand. "We love you too," she said. Then we ordered black beans and nachos. I don't remember much beyond that, just that the evening was fun and relaxing and that Wendy and Lisa were just as fabulous as I'd hoped, even without the teased hair and makeup. The artists of my teenage years might have gone on to other things, and the airwaves might be ruled by new names and new faces, but I still had *my* MTV, and it was every bit as wonderful as I had always thought it was.

The Condensed History of Gay Pride

It has recently been brought to my attention that a great many people are unaware of the history of our community. I made this amazing discovery while standing on the sidewalk watching our local Pride parade. As the Dykes on Bikes roared past, breasts to the wind and mirrored sunglasses glinting in the morning light, a young man to my right sporting rainbow-colored running shorts and a pink tank top turned to his friend and said, "I wonder how all of this started anyway." His companion took a sip from the rainbow-colored bottle of spring water in his hand and said, "I'm not sure. I've been coming ever since I was a kid. I just assumed it had always been going on."

Ah, the innocence of youth. Could it possibly be that there really is a generation of gay people who don't know why once every year we hold Pride celebrations all across our fair land? Why, Pride is the single biggest party of the queer calendar. It is our Christmas, our Fourth of July, and our Halloween all rolled up in one. It's the one day a year we get to take center stage and have ourselves a big old whoop-de-doo. Not knowing about Pride is like not knowing how to cruise. For any self-respecting gay person, it's unthinkable.

Clearly this ignorance of our heritage cannot remain unaddressed. If you don't know where you come from, you can hardly be expected to know where you are going. And as even the quickest of glances will reveal, the changing face of Pride is a reflection of the changing face of queer life. In its pageant of banners and signs, its people and its music, we see our dreams and our joys, our accomplishments and our challenges.

So, in the spirit of education, I offer this handy time line of Gay Pride, from its origins to its present. My hope is that it will enlighten the uninformed and remind the already-aware of what we have achieved and what we have yet to do. Remember, to know Pride is to know ourselves.

1543 B.C.: The residents of Sodom and Gomorrah hold a spontaneous weeklong orgy. When one enthusiastic participant runs through the streets waving a cum rag over his head, it is mistaken for a parade and an annual event is born. Sadly, its history is short-lived due to an Act of God.

1542 B.C.—1968 A.D.: Referred to by historians as The Time of No Floats, this dark period in gay culture saw very little in the way of organized events for queer people. Occasional parties and festivals were attempted but were generally not well-attended because of little inconveniences like the Bubonic Plague, the Inquisition, and the inability of the Merrye Gaye Fellowes Chorus and Chamber Orchestra to agree on an arrangement of "My Lover is the Sweetest Fruite" for their subsequently canceled spring concert.

1969: The birth of a new era. Following the historic Stonewall riots, everyone is filled with the power of liberation and a celebration is planned. When it is pointed out that late fall is hardly the time to be marching in the streets shirtless, the event is rescheduled for the summer of 1970, giving participants time to pump up and tan adequately.

1973: Thanks to the sponsorship of alcoholic beverage companies, gay pride events become a bit too reminiscent of the whole Sodom and Gomorrah thing. When shocking images of drag queens and leathermen appear on the evening news and frighten viewers, organizers decide to capitalize the name of the event—Gay Pride—to make it seem like a movement and thereby gain some legitimacy. Feeling left out, lesbians everywhere refuse to participate, but no one notices.

1974-1979: Considered by many to be the shining moment in the history of Gay Pride, the details of this happy period are nonetheless shrouded in mystery, primarily because everyone involved was too stoned to work their cameras properly. However, the by-products of this time, which include pierced nipples, the porn star as celebrity, and a renewed sense of humor, can still be felt today.

1980: Following the death of disco, Gay Pride organizers worry that attendance will drop. Fortunately, increased oppression provides a new theme, and the focus shifts from parades to rallies featuring long-winded speeches by hitherto unknown people about how being disliked really sucks. Lesbians everywhere enthusiastically applaud the decision, but no one notices.

1987: After several "downer" years marred by the AIDS crisis, Gay Pride festivities pick up steam again with the introduction of I'M NOT GAY BUT MY BOYFRIEND IS T-shirts, the "We're Here, We're Queer, Get Used to It" chant, and the mysterious ability of Alicia Bridges to appear simultaneously at every single parade singing "I Love the Nightlife."

1993: The era of political correctness. After voting to change the festival name to Gay, Lesbian, Bisexual, Transgendered, Transsexual, Queer, and their Friends, Families, and Supporters Pride, organizers panic when they realize the new name cannot be easily emblazoned on pins and T-shirts. Like Madonna and Cher, the name becomes, simply, Pride. Feeling left out, lesbians everywhere refuse to participate, but no one notices.

1997: Those born after Stonewall, annoyed at having missed out on all of the good drugs and easy sex, attempt to make up for it by creating 'zines and poetry slams expressing their angst. Their older brethren insist they have no sense of history and loudly cheer floats featuring members of Senior Action in a Gay Environment before attempting to pick up tricks from the queer youth contingents.

2000: Having become "just like everyone else," Pride celebrants are no longer distinguishable from straights. Many onlookers at the New York parade—dubbed

Pride?—believe the event, featuring grand marshals Bruce Bawer and Andrew Sullivan riding in a wood-paneled station wagon, to be a convention of Promise Keepers. Gay men who remember when Pride actually meant something join the lesbians and refuse to partici-pate, but no one notices.

Gym Dandy

I'm going to the gym again. I know, my past attempts at this have been disastrous. You don't have to remind me. But this time I think it will be OK.

I am doing this because I am in love, and being in love makes you do strange things like care about how you look naked. Being in love is a whole other story, and writing about it will have to wait until I've figured it all out. But it does have something to do with this gym business, so I thought it was only fair to mention it. Right now all you need to know is that his name is Dave and that he used to play football. This becomes important later on.

Historically, I have avoided the gym because it reminds me that I do not like my body. As it is hardly seemly to don, say, a parka when working out, you are instead forced to wear things like shorts and tank tops. This is all well and good if you look nice in such attire, but seeing that much of myself makes me more than a little uncomfortable. And we won't even discuss the horror of locker rooms and showers. Let's just say that they were bad enough in eighth grade. Twenty years later, everyone else still seems to have come along much more nicely than I have, and I resent it just as much now as I did then.

Nonetheless, I've been going dutifully every day and putting myself through the paces that my trainer, Brian, set up for me. Some of you might remember that I had another trainer, Paul, the last time I tried going to the gym. Well, I think I ruined Paul because he stopped training to become a physical therapist. He said at least in that line of work the people he's ordering around really have something to complain about. He said it in a very pointed way, which made me feel slightly guilty. But then I remembered I'd been paying him by the hour. When paying by the hour, one should be able to be as uncooperative and gloomy as one likes.

Brian has a different approach. The first time we met, he did a lot of measuring and wrote down how big my arms and chest and waist were and how much body fat I had. Then he made three columns next to those numbers and in them he wrote larger numbers (for the arms and chest) and smaller numbers (for the waist and body fat). "There," he said when he was finished. "Those are your three-month goals."

I looked at the numbers doubtfully. "You mean my arms will get that big in three months?" I asked.

"If you're a good boy and lift everything I tell you to they will," he said.

I like goals. And lists. I was one of those kids who raced through the variously colored reading booklets in elementary school one after the other just so I could check them off on my card and get to the end. I looked at Brian's numbers and immediately started wondering if I could get double the results by working out twice as much.

"No," said Brian, apparently reading my mind. "Don't even think about it. Just do what I tell you."

Sometimes it's a relief to be told what to do, especially if doing it means your arms grow by two inches and your body fat goes down five percentage points. So now every morning, before I'm awake enough to talk myself out of it, I show up at the gym and lift heavy things (well, fairly heavy things) for absolutely no reason except to change the way I look and to have the satisfaction of filling up the boxes on my compulsively organized workout record. People who need an excuse for such things like to pretend they're doing it because it makes them feel more alive, or because having greater strength means fewer back problems, or whatever. These people are liars. The only reason to lift weights is to make your arms and chest and other important parts bigger. Period. Sometimes when I'm lying there on my back trying to push some weight over my head, I realize how truly stupid it all is. But lately my arms have been getting a little bigger, and that, sadly, is all the incentive I need to go back and do it again.

Besides, I have had a small revelation that makes things easier. I've accepted that it's not so much that I don't like my body, it's that I'm not attracted to my body, or, more specifically, to other men who have the same body type. I have always wanted to be one of those really big, beefy guys with thick legs and arms like tree trunks. Somewhere along the line I convinced myself that because I happen to find those men attractive, I should make myself look like that too.

Well, I realize now this is not going to happen, even with two more inches around my arms. I have never weighed more than 175 pounds, and no matter how much I lift or eat, I do not put on weight or bulk up all that much. Working out gives me lots of definition and strength, but mass eludes me. As a result, my past work-out efforts have ended in frustration because, while it's nice to be able to lift heavy things with ease, it's nicer when your pecs look great under a T-shirt.

I blame this mental illness, of course, on being a gay man. Everyone knows that the first rule of gay dating is that you must stick to your own body type. Your part-ner should look almost exactly like you; at the very least you must have the same build. This is so both of you can feel secure about your looks and never wonder what the other sees in you. I encounter this a lot in the couples who come to the gym together. They are almost always interchangeable, from their matching outfits and weight belts to the amount of weight they can bench press. But because I have always been attracted to guys with almost the exact opposite of my body type, this has thrown the whole dating thing off course for me from the beginning.

This brings us back to me and Dave. Dave, as I men-tioned earlier, played football. He is a big boy. He is sev-eral inches taller than I am, and he outweighs me by a good 40 pounds. I love this about him. It's wonderful to have someone that big put his arms around me, and it's fun to watch people get out of the way when we walk around together.

I, on the other hand, am built for other things. As I said to Dave the other day, "Men like you were made to tackle other men, and men like me were made to run away very quickly from men like you." Bulk versus

quickness is nature's way of evening things out, a lesson
I have learned from watching animal documentaries on
cable. Lions may be big and strong, but their favorite
food is able to run like hell when they see the big cats
coming. It's only fair.

Only I'm not running away. Despite the gay dating
rules, Dave and I managed to get together, and neither
of us is going anywhere now that we've hooked up. The
fact that he is attracted to me is very reassuring. It's also
a bit bewildering. But I'm getting used to it, and less
and less I wonder when I'm going to find out it's all a
big joke, which has helped me view working out in a
different light. Now, instead of getting frustrated that I
can't look just like the guys I find really hot, I've started to see there are men who like the kind of guy I am
just fine. I don't know why this never occurred to me
before, but it didn't. Probably because I was too busy
blaming my tall, thin Irish ancestors for not having
beefier genes.

So bit by bit I'm getting over this body image issue—
at least a little. I still want to be bigger. I still feel deflat-
ed when I finish working out and someone comes along
and ups the weight I was just lifting by three billion
pounds. And I still look at the big brutes pumping huge
amounts of weight over their heads and envy their size.
But now I can enjoy watching them without getting mad
about the fact that I can't be one of them. It helps that I
have Dave to remind me—usually without any prompt-
ing on my part—that he likes the way I look. And last
week one of the oxlike guys with a body I've always lust-
ed after came up to me in the locker room and said, "You
have the nicest ass I've ever seen. I'd kill to have a butt

like that." Finally, after 20 years, I felt the weight of all those awful gym class memories slip away.

Odd Ducks

At one of the ponds my dog Roger and I like to walk around in the mornings, there is a small flock of ducks. There's nothing especially interesting about that; where there's water, there are ducks. But this particular group of ducks is different in that it's made up of five members—two male-female couples and one lone male. Ducks always pair up, so it surprised me the first time I saw the solo male swimming behind the two couples.

At first I assumed that his mate was just paddling around somewhere else or off building a nest or chasing the ducklings around. But day after day I would see the fivesome trolling around in the reeds or treading water, tails-up, as they nosed around in the pond grasses at the bottom. The lone male was definitely a bachelor.

Naturally, I wondered about the little male duck. What was his story? Was he the duck equivalent of the son who never left home? Had his mate been killed? Better yet, was he gay?

One of the arguments homophobes use to "discredit" gays and lesbians is that queerness does not appear in the animal kingdom, and is therefore unnatural. I always find this line of reasoning fascinating. I'm no expert on animal behavior, but I have a pretty good window into their world, particularly through the dogs in Roger's play group. And if canine behavior is any indication, humans aren't the only ones with a gay bent.

Take, for example, Stormy. Stormy is a big bitch. Literally. A cross between a shepherd and a husky, she's an enormously huge, enormously strong dog. Ever since she began coming to the park, she's been taking toys from the other dogs whenever she wants them and putting in their place any dogs foolish enough to put a nose near her butt.

At least until Patsy came along. Patsy is a dainty little black cocker spaniel. She couldn't hurt a fly if she threw all of her 20 pounds on it. Not that she ever would. It would mess up her fur.

The first time Patsy trotted into the park, Stormy charged over. Then, as we looked on in amazement, she rolled over, put all four paws in the air, and started licking Patsy's face. To the straight folks in the park, this was a miracle. Stormy had been transformed. But I'd seen it before. Stormy had simply met her femme. Now they're inseparable.

When Roger and I first started going to the park, Roger was enamored of a spunky mutt named Kendall whose name and appearance both provided no gender clues. As it turned out, Kendall was a female, and she and Roger formed a friendship that excluded all the other dogs. I confess that I was disappointed. But after a few months of hoping he might change, I accepted that my boy was heterosexual.

Six months ago Kendall moved away, breaking Roger's heart. For a long time he wouldn't even look at other dogs. He ignored their attempts to get him to play chase. He didn't join in the group roughhousing. He didn't want to walk around the pond with anyone but me.

Then Ezra came along. Ezra is a hunky 130-pound rottweiler with a spiked leather collar circling his tree-trunk neck. When he appeared at the park one evening, he and Roger eyed one another for an hour or so and then finally introduced themselves. They've been together ever since.

For the first time since Kendall's departure, Roger is a happy dog again. Whenever Ezra comes into the park, Roger runs over to meet him, tail wagging. Ezra's stumpy little tail wags back, and the two of them are off. It's quite a sight watching a huge Labrador and an equally huge rottie tear through a park, knocking each other over and pulling on one another's ears. Sometimes one of them will bring the other a ball or stick and lay it on the ground as a gift, looking on expectantly until the offering is accepted. Then it's all kisses and grunts.

Sometimes the two of them engage in more carnal delights, mounting one another clumsily with their big paws while their hind ends bounce back and forth futilely. There don't seem to be any particular rules to their amorous encounters, and neither seems to have a preference for who's on top. But if any other dog tries to hone in on the action, both Roger and Ezra growl and chase him or her away.

As you can imagine, I'm thrilled that Roger has found a boyfriend. Finally I can stop trying to hide his heterosexuality from my friends by saying that he "just hasn't met the right guy yet." Ezra's dad wasn't as thrilled. The first time he saw the two of them going at it, he tried to pull them apart and made all kinds of apologies for his son's behavior. "I don't know what's gotten into him," he said with embarrassment. "Maybe I don't play enough catch with him."

But slowly he's come to accept Roger and Ezra's relationship. He no longer tries to interest Ezra in the female dogs, and he even has a picture of the two boys sharing a stick taped to his refrigerator. When a visitor to the dog group saw Roger and Ezra playing and asked if they were related, I was proud to hear him say, "No, Roger is Ezra's special friend."

As for that little bachelor duck, I feared he would have to spend the long New England winter all by himself. Maybe the other ducks would invite him to holiday dinners and introduce him as "funny Uncle Walter" or something, but it wouldn't be the same as having his very own mate.

Then, a couple of days ago, another flock of ducks landed on the pond. Like the first group, there was a lone male among them, a shiny black and brown guy with a handsome purple band around his throat. He shook his tail feathers and swam around proudly.

This morning when Roger and I walked by, accompanied by Ezra and his father, most of that second flock was gone. But the original group was still there, the two males and the two females. And there, swimming along beside them, was the former bachelor duck and the purple-throated newcomer. The two males preened one another like any married duck couple, and the two hetero couples didn't seem to care one bit.

Odd ducks, all of us.

Size Matters

Researchers at the Kinsey Institute recently announced, after a study of some 1,500 male college students, that the length of the average man's penis has been downsized from 6.16 inches to 5.2 inches. As you can imagine, this reevaluation of the male member is of no little importance. Around the world, men are rejoicing in the fact that they have now become either closer to average or another inch or so beyond it. Not since the release of Viagra has male self-esteem been so high.

But I'm not so sure it's all good news, especially to those of us who have a special interest in male endowments. I am speaking, of course, of size queens. In the spirit of full disclosure I must confess that I am one. I know, it's shameful and wrong. But there you are. I like big ones. Not that I have anything against little ones, medium ones, or sort of big ones. They're all fine in my book, and I welcome their company. But the really big ones have a special appeal. And after years of exacting scientific research, I have come to one undeniable conclusion: Men lie about how big they are.

I have yet to meet the man who has never checked to see how he measures up. It's one of those things that guys just do, like drinking right out of the milk carton or not asking for directions. At some point in every man's life there is a moment when he just has to know how many inches he's packing. And, inevitably, he's disappointed by the results.

Before measuring, you can look at your pride and joy resting in your hand and think about how impressive it looks all puffed up and at the ready. But then out comes the tape measure and you realize that an inch is a lot longer than you thought it was. Staring down at the numbers, you convince yourself that surely something is amiss. Maybe the tape measure is defective? Perhaps it was manufactured in some foreign country that relies on the metric system and something was lost in the conversion? So you measure again. Maybe you try forcing more blood down there, hoping the exertion will push you past the magic number you have in your head. If that fails, there's always measuring from different angles.

According to the Kinsey researchers, however, the proper way to measure the length of a penis is along the top, from where it joins the body to the tip. I'm glad they set some ground rules about this, because some of the men I know have been using other methods. One gentleman of my acquaintance claimed to log in at nine inches. After getting a look at him, I can assure you he fell short. Finally, after pressing, he admitted that he had measured along the bottom—apparently starting at his prostate. "Maybe the tape measure slipped back a little," he said sheepishly as I docked him three inches.

This obsession with how big a guy is starts, as most truly important things in a man's life do, when he begins taking showers in gym class. Unless he has brothers who run around the house naked, or stumbles across a copy of *Playgirl* hidden beneath his sister's mattress, a young man doesn't have many opportunities for seeing penises other than his own. But once the gym shower comes into his life, perhaps in fifth or sixth grade, he becomes very much aware that all men are not created equal.

If a boy is heterosexual, he might not pay much attention to the genitals swinging all around him. Probably he takes a cursory look, sees how he compares, and leaves the locker room either envious or proud. But unless he is particularly large, and decides to announce it to the world by forcing his friends to call him "Horse," he most likely will not dwell on what he sees there.

For a budding queer boy, however, this first trip to the gym showers is a moment of unforgettable importance. He gets to see his classmates in their true glory, and he quickly learns that length and girth have a decided impact on how he views other men in relation to himself. Seeing that the school bully barely makes it past the two-mark may give him the confidence (and ammunition) he needs to stand up for himself the next time he's called a sissy. Getting a long look at a teammate's impossibly huge erection (caused, of course, solely by the hot water and not by any possible sexual thoughts) he may decide to extend that camping trip invitation after all.

If the locker room at my local YMCA is any indication, things do not change all that much as we age. The guys with the big ones still linger under the spray, gently soaping their privates as though waxing the most expensive luxury car. Their admirers hover nearby, casting longing glances or, unable to contain themselves, offering to lend a hand. In the changing area, it is not uncommon to find yourself holding your breath in anticipation as a long-admired fellow removes his shorts and slips off his boxers or briefs and you find out whether his reality measures up to your fantasy. Or maybe that's just me.

For size queens, the biggest controversy surrounding this average length question concerns the descriptive phrase "well-hung." Carrying a sense of mystery and adventure, this classification can elicit enthusiastic reactions when used judiciously in personal ads, general conversation, and chat rooms of the sexual variety. But without strict definition it can be misused by those who are either woefully misinformed or simply trying to get away with something. Many men have responded to the lure of "well-hung," only to find the user of the phrase has apparently compared himself only to four-year-old children and miniature dachshunds.

For most of us, the designation "well-hung" implies that the user's penis stretches significantly past average. But how far is far enough, especially now that the Kinsey people have lowered the bar? Is a man hefting 10.3 inches of joy more well-hung than one waving 6.9? Or is it simply a question of degree, with anything over 5.2 being technically equal to 11.8? You can see the dilemma, and those of us concerned about this matter are lobbying hard for clarification.

Frankly, I think this decreased penis length figure is all a new marketing strategy. Penises don't seem to be getting any smaller to me. But condom manufacturers have long known that making men think they're bigger than they are will increase sales. So they make their regular condoms smaller, forcing their once average-size customers to now buy the "King-Size" and "Magnum" varieties, and gladly. What guy wouldn't be proud to slap a box of "Stallion Super-Duper Extra Wides" on the checkout counter? So what if the contents are the same six-inch condoms found in the plain blue box he was mortified to be seen buying last week? Clearly, Kinsey and company are in on this.

This obsession with size isn't very healthy, and I admit that bigger doesn't always mean better. I've met more than one well-endowed fellow who thinks he's done his duty simply by showing up. This type generally lies back as if you've come for an audience with the Pope, waiting for you to kiss it and ask for a blessing. And there are other issues as well. I once dated a wonderful fellow who was absolutely huge. The only problem was, it took most of the blood in his body to maintain an erection. Whenever he got hard, his eyes glazed over, and getting him to process even simple sentences was impossible. I was always afraid that in his effort to keep it up he would pass out and I'd have a lot of explaining to do to the paramedics.

Despite these problems, I'm still fond of the big guys. And in the end, I suppose men can call themselves whatever they want. It's not as if you can hide a length deficiency when the actual unveiling comes. And really, once you've gotten to that point, how many men are actually going to get up and leave because of a slight size exaggeration? I know I wouldn't. Probably. But be warned: Until there's a stricter rating system, I'm carrying around a tape measure, and I know how to use it.

Getting Personal:
A Beginner's Guide to
Advertising for Love

In these busy days when most of us don't have time to
floss or eat breakfast, let alone search for our soul mates,
the man looking for love has to use every means at his
disposal. More and more, this means placing personal ads
in newspapers or on online bulletin boards. In an adver-
tising-oriented society in which catalog shopping has
replaced casual strolls through the mall, many men are
only too happy to embrace this new manifestation of the
mating dance. Just like choosing a J. Crew sweater and
ordering it with complete confidence that it will arrive
within 24 hours, we can sit in the comfort of our own
homes—while wearing our boxer shorts with the holes
in them—and pick out the man of our dreams as easily
as me might throw a box of cereal into the grocery cart.
So too can we put our own merchandise up for sale and
wait for the offers to come pouring in.

Despite the many wonderful opportunities afforded
by personal ads, however, there remains one big problem. No matter how easy the system may be to use, it still
depends on the ability of those who utilize it to come up
with raw material. Yes, even though you can put your ad
out there within moments, you have to write it first. And

as any casual glance through a typical personals section will prove, there is a talent to crafting the right sales pitch.

I happen to have some experience in this area, having placed a few ads of my own over the years. No, you're right, none of them resulted in a long-lasting relationship. Thank you for noticing. But they did teach me a few things about what to do and what not to do. And because I am always thinking of the welfare of others, I have developed the following helpful suggestions.

Physical Description: OK, for most of us the whole physical attraction thing is pretty important. Whether you like it or not, many people are going to make the first cuts on their list of dating prospects by weeding out those who don't meet their basic requirements in the looks department. That means you need to put it all right up front and get it out of the way. "GWM, 42, 6' 3", 195, br/bl, hairy chest" is a succinct example. Those interested in such a man will read the rest of your ad. Those looking for someone shorter, taller, heavier, thinner, blonder, green-eyed, or hairless will move along.

Remember, though, that there are a lot of 6' 3", 195-pound, br/bl men running around, and they all look very different from one another. Therefore, you need to give a little more. "Pierced nips" or "tattoo of Mighty Mouse across back" paints a more vivid picture, as does "shaved head" or "beehive hairdo." "Identical twin of Dennis Quaid" is sure to please, at least if I'm reading your ad.

Yes, there is room for error. In the case of pounds, you may be forgiven for adding or subtracting up to ten of them. But anything more than that is pushing it. Height is decidedly more difficult to fake. You can always squeeze your 36 waist into a pair of 34 jeans, but it's difficult to pull off 6' 1" when you're 5' 9". People notice.

Be wary, also, of using vague terms to describe your body type. "Athletic" applies equally to rugby players and ballet dancers, but those interested in one might be disappointed to see you're really the other. "Husky" is another frequent cause of unpleasantness. A big-boned boy with a body reminiscent of a prize steer has little in common with a gentleman whose girth exceeds his height due entirely to inactivity and overconsumption of packaged Hostess products. Be specific. After all, "in shape" does not necessarily mean that the shape is pleasing.

Photos: If your ad appears in a newspaper or magazine, chances are there will not be a photo accompanying it unless you happen to be the centerfold, in which case you should avoid talk of your interest in kittens and world peace and let the facts speak for themselves. However, if you are posting your ad to one of the numerous electronic areas that have been created for such things, you will likely have the opportunity to include a picture. If you decide to do this, keep in mind that it will be the first visual people will see of you, meaning it should make them want to see more of you. Under no circumstances should you use an image in which you are posing with an animal character at a theme park, being arrested at a demonstration, or dressed as Carol Channing. Other no-nos include photos in which your ex-lover appears with his face scratched out, and shots that include friends more attractive than yourself.

When considering the use of nude photos (assuming,

again, that you are not the centerfold) it is wise to remember that unless you have a remarkably large or attractive penis, most of them look pretty much the same and you should perhaps emphasize another of your assets. Also keep in mind that using a photo of a celebrity—even if everyone says you look just like him—is only going to attract stalkers who can't afford to fly to Hollywood to get the real thing.

Language: General descriptive terms are also potential stumbling blocks. There are, I admit, frequently acceptable variations in how different people define the same word. For instance, I concede that it is fine for two people to use the word *nice* in ways that might not at first seem entirely linked. One may think a *nice* day is one in which the sun shines steadily and the skies are blue. Another's *nice* day may be one in which no editors call demanding long overdue manuscripts. But to the individuals in common both are, essentially, the same thing.

The same cannot be said of words used in personal ads. Take, for example, the word *handsome*. It is undoubtedly a popular one, but I fear that it has, through overuse, become almost meaningless. The problem is that nearly everyone is handsome to someone. But if that someone is your mother—and no one else—it does little to snare the man of your dreams. The same goes for *all-American*, which means one thing to someone interested in frat boys and quite another to the guy with a membership in the Aryan Youth movement. *Boy next door* is to be avoided at all costs unless the person claiming it has a loft beside Ben Affleck's.

Another descriptive term that should be used with

caution is *romantic*. One man's *romantic* involves flowers, a candlelight dinner, and a sweet kiss good night. Another's involves a hockey game, several jumbo-size beers, and a handjob in the front seat. So think twice. Adding *hopeless* to this designation is precisely that.

Forbidden Words: It is wise for those writing personal ads to avoid certain terminology. Chief among these taboo words is *lonely*. If you are lonely, you are not going to remedy that situation by telling everyone that you have no friends and can't get a date. If being depressed and gloomy were attractive, you wouldn't be lonely in the first place. Admitting to such a thing is like advertising a used car and stating that it has "only been in three major accidents."

Other words and phrases to avoid include, but are not limited to, *codependent*, *parole*, *unemployed*, and *fungal infection*.

Especially Good Words: As disappointing as it might be to have to avoid certain words, the good news is that by including a few upbeat choices you can greatly increase your chance of success. There are many words which, when thrown into an ad at strategic points, are sure to attract potential lovers. For example, what man wouldn't stop to read more after seeing the word *heir*? Even if the only thing you're an heir to is your family's trailer in Ft. Lauderdale, at least you've gotten their attention, and it's a start. You can worry about the details later.

Other words and phrases almost certainly guaranteed to work in your favor include: *country house*, *CEO*,

Academy Award winner, and *former marine*.

Reveal Just Enough: Many people, when composing personal ads, feel the need to give fair warning about what prospective beaus are getting into. Perhaps thinking that honesty is the best policy, they announce that they "fall in love too easily" or "aren't always perfect," hoping the admission of these faults will be taken for eccentricities or endearing traits. This is the equivalent of a "buyer beware" sticker, and it doesn't work any better when selling yourself than when selling your home. While you might think your quirks will grow on someone over time, you don't have that much time. And no matter how nicely you put it, nobody likes a bed-wetter.

This is not to say that you should lie. In fact, creating a new persona for your ad is frowned upon. You might very well want to be a "mountain-climbing, foreign-film–loving photojournalist," but I assure you that you will not have enough time to transform yourself from the Saturn-driving, golf-playing insurance adjustor you really are before it's time to meet the guys you're trying to impress.

Know Your Audience: Second in importance to describing yourself is describing exactly what you want in return. "GWM seeks man" is hardly going to do the job unless you really don't care what you end up with, in which case you should turn immediately to the escort advertisements.

For the rest of you, ensuring that the responses you get come from men you might actually want to meet means ordering correctly. When you compose your ad, imagine that you're speaking to a waiter who will repair to the back for a bit and return with precisely what you asked for. Just as you'd hardly like to end up with chicken Kiev after requesting salmon steak with lemon-rosemary butter, you do not want to find yourself eating a slim redheaded botanist when what you're really hankering for is a blond, muscle-bound construction worker.

To avoid this, put what you want right up front and don't beat around the bush. "In search of a man who makes me laugh" could net you Drew Carey or Carrot Top, so be more precise. "Overgrown Boy Scout working on his merit badge in love seeks skinny skateboard punk into cheap beer and arson" is more to the point, and "Optimistic writer looking for dark-haired professional baseball player with big hands, huge dick, and three-year guaranteed contract" works well for everyone.

Take a Position: Knowing what you want is especially crucial when advertising for specific sexual needs. If you're a confirmed top or bottom, then say so. Finding a hot guy to hang out with won't do you much good if, when you get into bed, you fight over who will stick what where. "Aggressive top interviewing sissy bottoms into cleaning my house while wearing lederhosen" says it all, and "Versatile fireman at home putting out your fire or sliding down your pole" makes the picture more than clear.

If your tastes run to the exotic, then specificity is key. Ads containing words such as *vinyl pants*, *enema*, and *catcher's mask* will not escape the notice of those with similar interests. Now is not the time to decide to be experimental, so use them only if you're absolutely sure.

Now that you know the basics, you're well on your way to personal ad success. No, nothing can guarantee that the ad you ultimately come up with will net you the man of your fantasies. But it's certainly worth a shot, and by following the simple rules outlined above you're ahead of the game. So go on. Take a chance. If you get lucky, I'd be happy to help you write the vows for your commitment ceremony.

Runaway Train

There is an inherent danger in dating writers that stems from the fact that we are people who are used to dealing with an infinite range of possibilities. In our work we have to be able to imagine many outcomes for any problem our characters might face. Consequently our minds, either through training or natural inclination, can generate a shocking number of ways to deal with any situation we might find ourselves in. This can be a positive trait. Sometimes. For example, writers are more willing than most to hold romantic notions about finding true love and living happily ever after, if only because we have read far too many fairy tales.

But this ability to consider a range of options for any given situation can also lead to trouble, especially if, as I tend to be, the writer in question is drawn to the grimmest and most dramatic of options. In this case, an overactive imagination can turn a perfectly reasonable situation into an emotional meltdown. This is especially true when it comes to relationships, which tend to be touchy areas for writers anyway because we spend far too much time thinking about such things while avoiding deadlines.

Case in point: On Tuesday, Dave did not call me all day. For most people, this would probably not be a huge deal. Some people might not even notice if their boyfriends didn't call them for 24 hours. But I'm used to hearing from him at some point during the day, so I started to wonder. I tried not to wonder too much—I know how I can get—but by late afternoon I couldn't help having a couple of passing thoughts as I pretended to distract myself by working halfheartedly on a manuscript.

I started small. *Maybe*, I thought breezily, *he's busy working on something himself and just hasn't had time to pick up the phone*. That made me a feel a little better. For two seconds.

Of course, I couldn't leave well enough alone. That would be too easy. And emotionally healthy. Instead, I went for the more familiar option: I fretted. There is a scene in one of the *Winnie the Pooh* books in which the perpetually bitter donkey, Eeyore, is annoyed at the perpetually optimistic Piglet and Pooh for assuming that a tenuous situation they are all involved in will come out just fine in the end. "Think of all the possibilities before you settle down to enjoy yourselves," Eeyore says gloomily. And this is what I did. I did it all evening, while I waited for the phone to ring.

After it became clear to me that Dave and I had absolutely no psychic link whatsoever because if we did he would have felt me staring sorrowfully at the phone and picked it up to call me immediately, I decided to go to bed. Sleep is a great way for me to avoid this kind of mind game, as I can channel the extra worry into my dreams and pretend it's all just some healthy process of filtering out my neuroses. Besides, Dave frequently calls late at night so we can talk without interruption, and this way I could be unconscious while waiting.

This turned out to be a fine idea. I was so tired from all the fretting that I passed out quickly and went into a deep sleep—until I woke up for no reason whatsoever, rolled over, and saw that it was 1:37 in the morning. And, of course, the first thing that popped into my head was that I still hadn't heard from Dave. Fumbling in the dark, I picked up the phone and checked for the telltale beeping that indicates a waiting message, hoping maybe I'd been so tired that I just hadn't heard the phone (located two inches from my head) ringing. Hearing only the ugly, flat drone of a dial tone, I put it down, closed my eyes, and tried to go back to sleep quickly before my brain started functioning fully and ruined things utterly.

Too late. My imagination had already kicked in. And as every first-rate worrier knows, stewing in the middle of the night takes on a life of its own. Suddenly I found myself writing a screenplay all about the reasons for Dave's silence. It went something like this:

Dave is out on a date with someone else. He didn't call all day because he knew I would be able to tell that he was up to something. He's tired of our relationship and has decided to sow his oats elsewhere, or at least have a fling. Fine. Let him do that. I don't care. Oh, who am I kidding? Of course I care. But who might he be out with? Does he look like me? Is he better in bed? Who can I go out with to get even?

Or worse, Dave is lying in a hospital bed. A careless driver has crashed into him. The car was totaled. Jaws of Life were involved. There were many paramedics, all shouting, just like in ER. He's in a coma and no one knows to call me because he hasn't remembered to give my number to any of his friends, as I've asked him to many times. And I don't know any of their numbers either so I can't even call them to ask which hospital he's in. I wonder if the operator would connect me to all the emergency rooms in town? But what if I don't find him? It could be weeks, months, before I know what happened. And what if he's dead? I'll be a widow. How long do I have to wait until I date again, and will that hot guy who smiled at me at the gym want to go out with me if he knows my last lover died tragically? Or would it be more satisfying to grieve for a really long time and never love again?

Or Dave has merely fallen asleep while watching televi-sion and forgotten to call me. He is sleeping peacefully, snor-ing in that way of his that I usually find so adorable but now resent more than anything I can think of while I lie in bed and worry myself sick. How could he? Doesn't he know I'm waiting to talk to him? Doesn't he understand that when you say "I'll call you later tonight" to a writer, what the writer hears is "I will call you before midnight because at one minute after midnight it is tomorrow and therefore no longer 'later tonight' "? Doesn't he need me as much as I need him? Is he doing it just to make me mad?

I hoped he was having nightmares.

I looked at the clock again. It was 1:39. In the span of two minutes I had gone from being horribly jealous to horribly concerned to horribly vexed—a new world record in anxiety. But still the phone didn't ring, even when I counted backwards from 300, telling myself if everything was all right Dave would call before I got to zero. I dawdled on three, two, and one, drawing them out as long as possible, but nothing happened. Finally, I turned on the light, picked up a book, and read until I fell asleep again a few hours later. Then, only moments after I dozed off, it was time to wake up and walk the dog.

You might be wondering why I didn't just pick up the phone and call him. Well, that's easy. It would take all the fun out of everything. Plus, if I'd done that, Dave would have known I was worrying, and I couldn't have that. It's one thing to be mentally unwell; it's quite another to prove it to those who suspect it might be true.

He did finally call, the next afternoon. And, of course, as soon as I heard his voice I was fine. It turned out he hadn't called because he'd gone to a late movie with a friend and didn't want to wake me when he got home. Never mind that 12 hours before I would have given anything for him to have woken me up. It was suddenly as if the entire previous day had never happened and I was right back where I'd started, blissfully in love with the most wonderful man in the world. I couldn't believe I'd let myself get so worked up about nothing.

"I'll call you later," Dave said before we hung up, "and I love you." It doesn't get much better than that, and it was just what I wanted to hear from him. I hung up and went back to work, laughing at how silly I'd been. Then, about half an hour later, I looked up from where I was happily pecking away at my keyboard and found myself thinking, *I wonder if he meant he loves me like he loves his favorite shirt or he loves me so much he can't possibly live without me?*

Not What the Doctor Ordered

What is it with straight people thinking they have it so good?

In a recent broadcast of her popular radio show, Dr. Laura Schlessinger, known to her legions of fans as simply "Dr. Laura," uttered the now-infamous line, "Hear it one more time, perfectly clear: If you're gay or lesbian, it's a biological error that inhibits you from relating normally to the opposite sex."

Ignore for a moment that, as a counselor, Dr. Laura should have a slightly more informed view on sexuality. That's not really the point, because her views on most things pretty much originate in the thought processes of the Middle Ages. What's more intriguing is the motivation behind her statement. For if Dr. Laura is to be taken seriously, one has to accept her unspoken belief that heterosexuality is the pinnacle of human existence.

This is intriguing, because if you look at heterosexuality, it's not particularly enticing as a way of life. Granted, it *is* the most popular form of behavior on the planet, but that's not saying much when you consider that many of its adherents are the same people who voted for Reagan and consider golf an actual sport. I don't know about you, but as far as I'm concerned, wood-paneled station wagons, all-you-can-eat fish fry, and family vacations to the Grand Canyon do not a paradise make. I much prefer a Saab convertible, sushi dinners, and summers in Provincetown.

Besides, I don't have any problem relating to the opposite sex. I think women are great. Some of my closest relationships are with women. Sure, I know a lot of gay men who don't have any women in their lives except Streisand and Midler. And I know a lot of lesbians who won't give anything with a penis the time of day. But I know just as many straight women who won't talk to men either, unless they want help carrying in the groceries. And I can't think of any straight men who would happily go shoe shopping with a gal pal.

So if Dr. Laura's idea of "normal" relations between men and women comes down to being sexually aroused by the opposite sex, then no, I don't meet her criteria. But why not say heterosexuality is a biological error that inhibits people from relating normally to the same sex? Sure, many heterosexual women have women friends they're close to. But would they really watch their backs during a rugby scrimmage? And how many heterosexual men do you know who do much with their male buddies besides drink beer and talk about women they'd like to "relate" to? If that's normal male bonding behavior, I'll stick with the abnormality of Oscar parties, art openings, and having intelligent conversations over brunch.

I suppose Dr. Laura would argue that this is all *our* fault. After all, if straight guys weren't so afraid of being mistaken for gay, maybe they would help each other find pants that make their asses look better. But I doubt it. For one thing, I've met more than one "straight" man, complete with wife and kids, who goes in search of man-on-man action when he wants to really get it on. And I have many straight women friends who would take a banana split with chocolate fudge sauce over a penis any day. The old hetero thing might be fine when you want to be accepted socially, but when it comes to expressing sexual desire, it's another matter altogether.

So if we can remove attraction from the equation, maybe we can revise our thinking even more and say heterosexuality is simply a biological formula for the continuation of the species. This works for me, but in this age of donors and turkey baster babies, it's a definition that's teetering on the brink of obsolescence.

No wonder Dr. Laura is so afraid of us. No wonder she's claiming we're aberrations. Imagine how her theory would hold up if we were able to eradicate ignorance and prejudice. If society were freed of restrictions and we were all free to pair up with whomever we really wanted, would people conform to the "norm" of heterosexuality? Sure, some would. Maybe even a lot would. But I suspect the majority would fall along a spectrum, neither completely one thing nor another.

In the meantime, we still have folks who think being straight is some kind of paradise. I don't know why. I mean, if you actually do a side-by-side comparison of gay life and straight life, I don't think there's any question about which is preferable. I offer the following examples:

Products of Heterosexuality	Products of Homosexuality
Divorce lawyers	Great sex
Cruise ships	Cruising
Dysfunctional families	Chosen families
Game shows	Drag shows
John Wayne movies	John Waters movies
Velveeta	Brie
Congress	The Greek Empire

I admit that thousands of years of heterosexuality have produced some good things. After all, where would we be without, well, um...gee, this is harder than I thought. Well, there's always art and fashion and music. Oh, no, I guess there isn't. Architecture, theater, and film? Nope. Now that I think of it, there isn't a lot about heterosexual culture that anyone would really miss if it disappeared now. The atom bomb? Religious intolerance? Astroturf? Doubtful.

What really surprises me isn't the assumption by heterosexuals that they have the best deal in town. Of course they're going to think that. People seldom go around beating them up for having children and blatantly holding hands in public. But I am surprised by the number of queers who buy into Dr. Laura's argument, whether they know it or not. I'm the first one to encourage diversity, and I don't insist on anyone being forced to act or live a certain way. But not being an opera-loving, disco-dancing, Armani-wearing queen doesn't mean you have to go to the opposite extreme and move to the suburbs and get a minivan. Unless you really like such things. But let's face it, no one does. Not even Dr. Laura.

More and more, queer people are indistinguishable from straights. Maybe it's unrealistic of me to think that the entire institution of marriage can be dismantled, but I can't accept that the alternative is to give in and do what Mom and Dad did because it's the best we can hope for. Yes, I understand the arguments about benefits and partner rights and privileges. But I'd rather not have them if it means buying into the notion that equality is based on pieces of paper and your tax filing status. I don't see how taking on the trappings of straight life does anything but reinforce the idea that we want to be just like them because it's a better way to live. More convenient, yes. Better, no.

Don't get me wrong. Straight people are fine. Some of my best friends are straight. And it's not their fault that some of their kind are bad apples any more than I'm responsible for NAMBLA or the Log Cabin Republicans. But I have no illusions that their lives are better than mine. In fact, they're often the ones to sigh wistfully and say, "Your life is so interesting." They're right. It is. Or it should be. But keeping it interesting means remembering that the things that seem like liabilities are really assets if you know how to embrace and celebrate them.

Dr. Laura frequently says that what we really need is a return to morals, values, and religion. I agree with her on the morals and values. I even agree with her on the need for religion. Sort of. But what Dr. Laura doesn't understand is that religion is only the outward expression of innate spirituality, and that any religion based on fear and easy answers is a weak one. True spirituality teaches acceptance of the Divine (or, if you're queer, the Fabulous) in all its forms, which is something Dr. Laura knows nothing about.

Nor does she understand that the morals and values we need are, quite simply, love and kindness, not an outdated ideal that never offered anything useful to begin with. Monogamy and commitment ceremonies are fine if that's what you want. I'll be the first to send you a toaster. But please don't think it means anything more because some pencil pusher at city hall put an official stamp on it. True commitment is found in living life together every day and staying together because it matters to you, not because coming apart would mean having to divvy up the CDs and the few paltry dollars in the joint checking account.

Maybe Dr. Laura does understand this, but because she is conveniently included within the majority that dictates how things should be, she prefers to keep things just the way they are. And it's not surprising that Dr. Laura's audience adores her. Because they are ignorant and confused, with lives so wildly dysfunctional that hearing Dr. Laura berate them for their stupidity gives them a giant jolt of self-esteem.

But you have to wonder about Dr. Laura herself. From her seemingly endless rage, it's clear that she gets little from "helping" her listeners. In many ways, she reminds me of the Christian God of my childhood— kindly when you agree with him, but willing to turn you into ashes if you dare say he isn't always right. Is it possible that, unhappy with her existence, Dr. Laura has chosen to take it out on those of us who are truly content? I hate to break it to the good doctor, but if what she is passes for normal, I'll happily stay in my sick bed.

Playing It Straight

A number of years ago I was asked to appear on a television talk show to discuss why so many people in the gay community have a problem with bisexuals. I don't remember why I was chosen to speak on behalf of annoyed queers everywhere, as I wasn't particularly bothered by bisexuals, but there you are. Probably I just thought it would be fun to be on television, or they promised me lunch or something. I do remember that I bought new shoes for the occasion.

When it was my turn to talk, I explained that a lot of gay people resent the fact that many bisexuals only consider themselves part of the queer community when they're in same-sex relationships and want the support of a larger group, but when they're involved with people of the opposite sex they forget all about the queer community and enjoy the privileges the appearance of heterosexuality affords. This went over very well with the large gay contingent in the audience, but the glamorous bisexuals on the panel, all of whom wore leather and sunglasses for some reason, pouted because they knew they'd been found out.

Well, now I feel just the tiniest bit guilty. You see, I've

been doing exactly what I accused those poor belea-
guered bisexuals of doing. Sort of. I'm not sleeping with
women, but I've been letting people think I am.

It's all because of Kyle, the sales clerk at J. Crew. A few
months back I had to buy some clothes for an event I was
attending, and I really didn't want to do it. I hate shopping, especially for clothes, and I always end up making
a disaster of it. As usual, I waited until the last minute.
I'd even tried to get picked for *Fashion Emergency*, that
show on E! where they take hopeless people and put
them in things that make them look slightly less hopeless. I'd written them a letter saying I'm a gay man who
can't dress. They never responded. They probably
thought it was someone trying to be funny.

With time running out and no options left, I was
forced to drag myself to the J. Crew store at our local
Mall of Hell. Malls make me nauseous, but the models in
J. Crew catalogs always look nice, so I figured I couldn't
go wrong. After all, how hard could it be to pick out
some pants and a shirt?

I should have known. As soon as I entered the store,
the familiar panic set in. There were too many choices,
too many colors and patterns and styles. I tried to focus
and remember the advice given to me by my mother,
who, when I was a teenager, became a "fashion consult-
ant" and spent many evenings draping everyone in the
family with variously colored swatches of material to
determine our "seasons" and thus the colors that would
look best on us. Unfortunately, I didn't fall neatly into
any of the categories. Instead of being a full-on winter or
summer, with their respective palettes of acceptable and
flattering hues, I was more of a late-March thaw, not

quite one thing or another. Clothes have been a night-mare ever since.

I wandered around the store for a while, wondering what might go with what, and then it all became too overwhelming. I started to leave. But as I raced for the exit, I was accosted by a smiling young man with perfect hair, perfect teeth, and perfect clothes. His whole being screamed "J. Crew!" He was clearly gay, and he knew how to dress. I wouldn't normally talk to such a person because doing so only magnifies my insecurities and makes me tense, but he was determined to make a sale.

"Good afternoon," he said. "I'm Kyle. Can I help you with anything?"

The smart thing to do would have been to mumble a quick "no, thank you" and run for my life. But I have a hard time saying no to salespeople. The word *commission* always flashes through my head, and suddenly I feel responsible for their well-being, like if I don't buy any-thing they won't be able to afford the liver transplant they so desperately need. But while I may feel slightly guilty, I don't make it easy for them.

"I'm going to this thing," I said unhelpfully. "I need to wear something."

Kyle looked me up and down. As usual, I was wearing old jeans, a flannel shirt, and work boots. I'd also thrown on a very worn and rather dirty canvas coat of the type favored by construction workers, and a baseball cap. All of these things had been worn earlier to take the dog to the park, and I was horrified to notice now that most of my lower body was covered in muddy paw prints and streaks of dirt where Roger and his friends had used my legs as napkins. Kyle took it all in and smiled.

"How about a suit?" he asked.

"Absolutely not," I said immediately. "I'd rather die."

"OK then," he said. "How about pants, a shirt, and a tie. Maybe even a jacket?"

That sounded better, even though in the back of my mind I suspected I was still getting a suit, just in pieces. But at that point I would have done anything to get out of that store. It was bad enough having to buy grown-up clothes, and having a fellow queen see the true depth of my fashion ignorance was too much.

"Do you have any idea what you might want?" asked Kyle hopefully.

I shook my head. "I really hate shopping," I admitted. "I mean *really* hate it. You have no idea."

Kyle nodded. "Let me guess, your girlfriend usually picks out everything for you."

"Girlfriend?" I said, confused.

"I'm sorry, your wife. I didn't notice a ring, so I assumed you weren't married."

It suddenly dawned on me then that Kyle thought I was straight. I started to laugh, and was about to correct him, when I was overcome by a horrible thought. He seemed to be enjoying helping out the poor straight guy with no fashion sense. Probably he saw me as his mission for the day. I doubted he would be as enthused about dealing with one of his own who was just too stupid to pick out clothes by himself.

"Oh, there's no ring," I said finally. It was true, if a tad misleading. It wasn't my fault if Kyle made the wrong assumption.

Kyle beamed. "Well, then, I'll have to see what I can do for you," he said.

For the next hour Kyle busied himself picking out clothes for me. He told me what pants looked the best, and what colors of shirts went with which ties. He fussed and straightened and buttoned until I felt just like one of the models in the catalog. He practically offered to come over and dress me the night of the event. When I left he assured me that he'd had a wonderful time. I felt as if I should say, "Me too. I'll call you."

I went home feeling awful about letting the poor man think he was doing a hapless straight boy a favor. But what little bit of guilt I felt over duping Kyle faded when everyone complimented me on my wardrobe later that week. So what if he thought I was straight? I looked great.

What I wasn't expecting, though, was the lure of heterosexuality. I confess that since Kyle I've done this several more times, with both male and female store clerks. Usually all it takes is me wandering into a store and looking around in a dazed manner. Inevitably someone comes along, takes me by the arm, and tells me exactly what I want. Just last week a charming young man spent a good 20 minutes picking out the perfect underwear for me. I can't tell you how relieved I was not to have to do it myself. Deciding between the jersey boxers and the button-fly shorts was more than I could handle.

I inevitably feel guilty when I pull off the straight routine. I swear each time that it will be the last time, just like I did with masturbation when I was 12. But then I find I can't pick out a decent pair of shoes, and before I know it I'm hinting to the salesman that my wife and I are going somewhere nice and I'm not sure what would go best with my brown pants.

Maybe I am a traitor to the cause. Maybe I'm just as horrid as those leather-wearing bisexuals hiding behind their sunglasses. Maybe someone should drag me on a talk show and tell the world my secret shame so I'll snap out of it and admit I'm a fashion troglodyte. I don't care. For the first time in years I match, and that's all that really matters.

It Is Hereby Resolved

As a rule, I do not like New Year's resolutions. If you're anything like me, they're essentially a guarantee that you begin your year with failure, thereby setting the tone for the next 364 days. And since most people do not think "watch more porn videos" is an acceptable form of the resolution, I no longer bother.

I wasn't always like this. When I was an adolescent I adored New Year's resolutions. The problem was, I had only one. Every year, as December 31 neared, I would decide that on January 1 I would awaken into a world free of my nastiest habit, masturbation, which I was convinced was the worst sin there was.

Thus resolved, I would spend most of the week between Christmas and New Year's locked in the bathroom, beating off furiously in a marathon masturbatory countdown while thinking ahead to the coming days of purity and goodness. After relieving myself, I could actually convince myself that I'd be able to keep my hands-off policy for the entire year. It seemed easy enough.

But, inevitably, it wasn't. The first day of January would come and go, and I'd be pretty much OK. Pleased with myself for sticking to my resolution for almost 24 hours, I would go to bed and rejoice in how good I was. Then, about five minutes later, I'd find my hand in my pajama bottoms. I would tell myself I was just going to prove once and for all that I could have a platonic relationship with my genitals. A little touching was OK, I reasoned, as long as there was no actual ejaculation.

Two hours later, as I ground my teeth and tried to will my erection away by repeating Bible verses over and over, I would realize I'd lost again. Before midnight came, I had as well. And, thus, my first day of the new year was soiled once again with the sticky evidence of my inability to maintain self-control.

After a few years of this annual disaster, I gave up resolutions for good. From time to time as I grew older I would half-promise myself that in the new year I would write every day, or maybe go running more than once a month. And sometimes I even managed to do those things, at least for a couple of weeks. Once I even made it to February 17. But that was the extent of it. No matter how much I wanted to change something in my life, it wasn't long before I was back to my selfish, slovenly ways.

The real problem, I've decided, is that I don't have enough vices. For a resolution to be successful, there has to be something sacrificed. But I don't smoke. I don't overdo it on gin and tonics. I don't snort illicit substances. I'm not addicted to anything, I go to bed on time, and I don't drink coffee. If I were grossly overweight, at least I could work on shedding those extra 50 pounds and watch with glee as my goal grew nearer. But, alas, there's not enough extra flab to last through more than a few weeks of dieting. Some people have suggested that cynicism and sarcasm are two of the ugli-est vices around, but I think they'd do well to consider nail-biting before they jump to conclusions.

Yes, I know that I could think of things to add to my life. But that's even worse. If I decide to start going to the gym, which would not be a bad thing, it just sets me up for another, slightly different kind of failure. The same with resolving to see my friends more, wear something other than jeans and T-shirts, or learn Italian. Each sounds fine in theory, but I know that sooner or later I'd resent the effort. Like the whole masturbation thing, I might be able to keep up with my new lifestyle for a short while, but as soon as I realized it was cutting into my nap time I'd have to stop. I prefer to simplify, not complicate, my daily existence.

Despite my aversion to the whole resolution thing, I still find myself yearning to get into the spirit of it all. I have tried to come up with ways to make it work for me. One idea I've toyed with is acquiring some really bad habits around November. Shooting heroin, for instance. If I started at Thanksgiving, by the time New Year's rolled around, I'd have a minor habit. Then I'd have something to give up. I'd feel better about myself, and any resulting physical or emotional damage would prob-ably be fairly minor. Similarly, I could begin smoking excessively in mid November. Not only would it come in handy at holiday parties, but I'd be glad to stop because I really hate the taste. Having successfully completed my one and only resolution, I would then be free to resume my normal life with renewed self-confidence.

As appealing as this plan is, I know it isn't going to happen. I don't know where to score heroin and I don't have the cash to purchase cigarettes in bulk. But I'm tired of looking toward the turn of the calendar with dread while all my friends launch themselves into a frenzy of self-improvement, so I have decided to take another, more useful approach. In the spirit of bettering myself, I have compiled a list of ten resolutions I feel will genuinely affect my life as a gay man in the coming year. Unlike the resolutions of years past, these ten goals are practical, and for once I am pretty sure I will stick to them. They are also free, and require no actual physical exertion, which is always a bonus.

Here, in no particular order, are my ten Resolutions for a Gay New Year. Feel free to adapt them for your own use.

1. I will not feel kindly about a straight celebrity just because he or she has gay friends or a gay child or once knew someone gay who died from AIDS. This resolution extends to refusing to read any gay magazine that thinks it is a good idea to slobber over straight "supporters" we are glad to have on our side. No amount of money or Oscars can make up for a person never having tasted the bodily fluids of someone of the same gender.

2. I will not read any gay novel in which the "middle-aged" main character turns out to be under 40. It's bad enough that, at 30, people are asking why I haven't written a screenplay yet. It used to be that no one even began their lives until their fourth decade. Now grade schoolers are having retrospectives. These people should remember that *Logan's Run* was not a comedy.

3. I will not take seriously the opinion of anyone who can name Madonna's last five singles and their peak chart positions. I like music as much as the next guy, but I can no longer pretend lyrics like "You're frozen when you're heart's not open" are worth crying over, or that putting together a song from bits and pieces is a talent. Some of us still remember Dusty Springfield and the live recording process.

4. I will not have as a friend anyone who really cares what Leonardo DiCaprio, Antonio Banderas, or Brendan Fraser are up to at any given moment. I will be the first to admit that celebrity is appealing, but at some point we must all realize that we are not going to run into any of these people on the subway and start relationships with them. The exceptions to this rule are, of course, Alec Baldwin and Bruce Willis, who I'm sure are just as nice as I think they are.

5. I will not watch any television show with gay characters and wish the straight actors were really gay. Nor will I watch *Buffy the Vampire Slayer* and wish I was Sarah Michelle Gellar. I do, however, reserve the right to fantasize about being Xena's friend, as I see no possible harm in it.

6. I will not wear any undergarment simply because I see it modeled in a magazine by men with bodies created by steroids and sock-enhanced crotches. Attractive underwear is nice, but let us not forget that underwear's primary function is preventing unsightly stains. And really, how many times will any of us find ourselves playing beach volleyball with a bunch of humpy guys in boxer briefs?

7. I will no longer persist in believing there are gay major league baseball players who secretly lust after my picture on my book covers and think I'm really funny. But if there do happen to be any, my editor will be more than happy to forward your letters. [Editor's Note: Unless you're Derek Jeter. Then I'm keeping you for myself.]

8. I will not pretend I think gay marriage is a great leap forward. Receiving a lot of appliances hardly makes up for playing by their rules, and if we start viewing the ability to file taxes jointly as a worthy achievement we will soon be making excuses for owning things like polyester pants and minivans.

9. I will not use the word *brunch* in a conversation. I am happy to eat eggs Benedict and talk about who slept with whom the night before, but there is absolutely no need to invent an excuse for getting up late on Sunday mornings.

10. I will remind myself on a daily basis that I do not have to put up with any grief from straight people just because there are more of them, nor from gay people just because they have more accessories.

Rite of Passage

Yesterday I became a man. It happened in the checkout line of Home Depot. I was standing there, waiting to pay for the brand new 18-inch Weber grill that sat in its box in my cart when a voice behind me said, "That's a fine grill you've got there."

I turned around. The speaker was a man in his 60s. He was wearing plaid shorts, a Red Sox T-shirt, and white socks. He appraised my grill and nodded approvingly.

"I've had my Weber for 30 years," he said. "You'll get a lot of use out of that baby if you treat her well."

Clearly this was a man who knew his stuff when it came to outdoor cooking. I patted the box, pleased that I'd made a good choice. "Yep," I said. " I can't wait to fire her up."

Something about that sentence struck me as familiar. Then it hit me: My father had uttered the exact same words 25 years earlier. I was five. We were standing in line at Dart Drug. It was summer. And he'd just purchased a new grill.

I still remember that grill. As soon as we got home, my father set it up in the backyard. He loaded it up with charcoal, ordered us all to stand back, and set a match to it. We oohed and aahed appreciatively as the flames leapt up, burned brightly for a few minutes, then settled down to a dull glow.

From that moment on, the grill was the center of my dad's universe. Every night that summer we waited expectantly as he stood over the fiery embers, turning the hot dogs, flipping the burgers, and moving the pieces of chicken to just the right spot to get the skin crispy while the inside stayed juicy. Like some kind of strange suburban alchemist, he mixed secret barbecue sauces and developed his own peculiar basting rituals for getting the various items just so.

My sisters and I were the beneficiaries of his mastery of the grill, and in those three months during the summer of 1973 we consumed more meat than an entire herd of wild dogs, falling upon his creations ravenously night after night. Bellies full to bursting, we would sleep contentedly, our mouths watering as we dreamed of steaks, rare and tasting faintly of ash.

The grill was my father's domain. The rest of us were forbidden to touch it or even to go near it. "Get away from that!" my father would shriek as one of my sisters attempted to take another hot dog on her own. Racing over, he would snatch the tongs from her hand. "You have to do it a certain way," he'd explain patiently, carefully lifting the frank and setting it on her plate like an angel descending from heaven. The message was clear: We were not worthy to attempt grilling ourselves.

I was not, of course, the only boy whose father knew the magic of the grill. All across my neighborhood were men who stood on patios at dusk, filling the skies with the thin smoke of roasting food. Their eyes all held the same faraway look, a pleasure bordering on madness, as they presided over their round, fiery kingdoms. For those of us who stood nearby and watched, the grills became Holy Grails, things we could spend a lifetime studying but never fully understand.

Sometimes during the day, while our fathers were at work, the boys of the neighborhood would congregate in a backyard. Unlocking the shed or garage where the grill of the house was kept, we would stand around it, looking at this symbol of manhood whose secrets were as yet unknown to us. Even empty of glowing coals they fascinated us. Their steel bowls held the promise of adulthood. The tools that hung from their specially designed racks—spatulas and tongs and extra-long forks—gleamed seductively. We dreamt of the day when they would be ours to wield.

Various cultures have their own special ways of marking the passing from childhood to adulthood. Some send the young person into the forest for a few days to fend for himself, armed only with his wits and maybe a length of twine. When he returns carrying a slaughtered wild pig on his back, he is welcomed as a man. Others mark the transition with dancing, drumming, and the ritual scarring of delicate body parts.

In our society the celebrations are usually less dramatic. Graduation parties. Trips to the mall for training bras or athletic supporters. The securing of the all-important driver's permit. Living rooms across America are filled with photos of children, long since grown, hoisting swimming medals in triumph, or standing next to prom dates whose ill-fitting tuxedos or broad swipes of blue eye shadow are the plumage of burgeoning maturity.

Although they might not be as splashy as the traditions of other cultures, these moments are nonetheless highlights of a person's life. Looking back, we can see each step we took as we grew closer to the time when we were no longer children. I have friends who remember the exact date and hour of their first pimple. My sister, now in her 40s, still talks nostalgically of the first time she used a tampon. Standing in the bathroom with one foot resting on the edge of the bathtub, she inserted the cardboard wand with trembling fingers and marveled at the mysteries of flowering womanhood.

Gay men, of course, are not exempt from these rites of passage. But for many of us, these modern-day manhood rituals are at least somewhat traumatic. The purchasing of a jockstrap, for example, may coincide with the discovery that one is not at all skilled in dribbling a ball from one end of a court to another. The first school social, carrying with it the necessity of asking a girl to attend, might bring terrors of enormous proportion. Rather than feeling the first stirrings of adult freedom, many gay men realize that they quickly need to develop a repertoire of excuses to explain why they prefer to stay home watching *Now, Voyager* to dancing the night away with their peers.

My own transition to adulthood went largely unnoticed. I stayed far away from school social functions, and left high school before graduation. My first shave occurred while I was at camp, without my parents to take note of it, not that I would have wanted them to. Because we lived in farming country, I was driving our truck long before I was legally allowed, and it was years before I got a proper license—and then only because I needed one for identification purposes.

For me, becoming an adult was a journey with murky road marks. One day I was playing with blocks; the next I was paying my own rent on a studio apartment in New York. It all happened very quickly, and my parents, not being particularly sentimental, have never offered any stirring memories of my change from boy to man. It just sort of happened. And somewhere along the line I forgot all about the grill. After all, gay men don't grill. We broil.

At least until yesterday. Warmed by the summer sun, I suddenly had a longing for a nicely grilled steak. Sure, using the oven would be easier. But I pictured myself standing by my grill, tongs in hand, and I liked what I saw. So off I trundled to Home Depot. It wasn't until I was in line and found myself discussing the merits of my new purchase that I thought of my father. When I did, I smiled to myself as I realized that finally, on the cusp of turning 30, I felt like a grown-up. And it had nothing to do with the IRAs I'd dutifully contributed to, the books I'd written, or the many other little trappings of adulthood that decorate my life. It was because I had my own grill.

I decided to invite my friend Jackie over to celebrate my manhood. A veteran of hundreds of post-softball game cookouts, Jackie is my one friend who I knew would truly appreciate the symbolic meaning of my first time overseeing the grill. After setting up the Weber, I filled it with charcoal and lit it, just as my father had before me. I waited patiently until the coals were glowing warmly, then brought out the platter of steaks. Lifting one gently with my new tongs, I set it onto the grill and heard the beautiful sizzle that heralded my newfound status. I felt like howling at the sky in some primal way.

My euphoria lasted approximately 30 seconds. Then Jackie came over and snatched the tongs from my hand. "Get out of the way," she said, setting her sights on my steak. "You're doing it all wrong."

Cheaper by the Dozen

Twice in the last month I have been asked if I would like to become a father. All of my lesbian friends are going baby-mad, and two different couples put out feelers to see if I might be interested in helping them produce additions to their families.

I'm honored to be asked, of course. It's nice to know that someone might want to take a chance on my DNA. And all it involves is a small jar, good aim, and the right moment. But I don't know. The last time I did this, it almost gave me a nervous breakdown.

I was 13. I know, that's a little young to be a dad. But it wasn't like I had a choice in the matter. It was either that or take a failing grade, and I figured having a kid would be easier to explain to my parents than an F on my report card.

It was eighth grade. Health class. We were discussing the responsibilities of parenting, which was a fairly relevant issue in my little country school where every year at least a handful of girls waddled down the aisle at commencement in maternity gowns. Our teacher, Mr. Travis, decided that we were taking the whole thing far too lightly and needed a lesson in the difficulties of having young ones to care for. So we all became parents for a week.

Our children were eggs. Mr. Travis set a couple of cartons of them on his desk and, one by one, we went up and claimed our babies. Returning to our seats, we held them anxiously while Mr. Travis explained what his little exercise entailed.

We were to keep our baby eggs for one week, naming them and decorating them in any way we saw fit. We could carry them around in any kind of conveyance we came up with, but we had to have them with us at all times. They couldn't sit in our lockers. And if we had to be involved in some activity that took us away from our charges—like gym class—we had to find a baby-sitter. At night, of course, we were allowed to refrigerate our charges, lest they become spoiled.

If we managed to make it through the week without any harm coming to our child, we would receive an A on the assignment. But if Friday dawned and our little one had become scrambled or cracked, we would get an F. It was that simple: pass or fail. There were no in-between grades. And because we had to decorate our eggs in some distinctive way, Mr. Travis would know if we cheated and substituted another one for a deceased child.

We took to the challenge with mixed emotions. Most of the girls thought it was great fun, while the boys looked at the fragile eggs cradled in their clumsy hands and immediately considered hard-boiling them to make them sturdier. This, however, was one of the many options forbidden to us. So we did the best we could, constructing all kinds of clever carrying cases for our progeny that would survive any catastrophe.

What we hadn't counted on, however, was the almost

irresistible appeal of infanticide. What started out as a well-intentioned exercise in parenting soon turned into a bloodbath as we discovered that finding ways to bring about the demise of the eggs of our friends and enemies was much more entertaining than minding our wards. By the end of third period we had our first casualty; Jason Pritchard tripped Louis Sutton on the way to algebra and little Louis Jr. fell headlong to the cold hallway floor, his yellow insides splattering the tile. We stared at the fragments of eggshell, and instead of feeling sorrow for Louis's loss, we immediately hatched evil plans of our own.

Like some kind of primal instinct, destroying other students' children became our foremost goal. Each of us wanted to be the last one standing come Friday. We lurked on stairs, pushed chairs into the paths of rival parents, and bumped into one another in the lunch line. The sound of an egg hitting the floor while a bereaved parent howled in anguish became music to our ears, and we chortled horribly whenever someone else bit the dust and our own eggs were still safe and sound.

My egg was named Rupert. He had a cheerful little painted-on face and he lived in a carriage made of styrofoam egg carton pieces, cotton, and lots of tape to hold him in place. While I confess I was concerned for his well-being more out of a desire to maintain a high grade point average than from any sense of paternal duty, I did care for him in my own way. I was careful to keep him with me at all times, eyeing anyone who came near me with suspicion. I even walked home with him every night, lest some bully on the bus kidnap him and pitch him out the window, as had happened to Anne Chattam one afternoon when she refused to hand over five bucks to free her precious Charlotte from the clutches of a tenth-grader.

By Wednesday, fully half the class had lost their egg babies to neglect, accident, or murder. There had even been one case of a hired nanny shaking an egg in her charge so badly that it cracked. She claimed it was the fault of a one-armed intruder, but none of us believed her.

On Thursday, the pressure intensified. Those without eggs decided the rest of us would join them in failure. It was an all-out slaughter. Eggs were ripped from their parents' arms and hurled against walls. Gangs of eggless thugs roamed the halls, descending on anyone foolish enough to get in their way. Some anxious kids tried to protect their offspring by sending them to live with younger siblings in the lower grades for the day. But that proved their undoing, as day care was strictly forbidden and Mr. Travis pronounced them unfit parents.

By Friday morning there were only two of us remaining. I had managed to keep Rupert unharmed largely because I'd asked my friend John Reynolds, a senior with a lot of muscles and a bad attitude, to be Rupert's godfather in exchange for my doing his English homework. My friend Carolyn also still had her egg, Mellicent, whom she had kept intact by threatening to report anyone who came near her to the principal, who also happened to be the egg's grandfather.

It was down to the two of us. This wouldn't have been a problem under normal circumstances, but Carolyn and I were always vying for the top spot in our class, and at that moment we were in a dead heat. Whichever of us was the best parent would be victorious. But when we both walked into class with our little ones in tow, it seemed we would have to settle for a draw.

When the moment came to present our healthy bouncing babies to Mr. Travis, Carolyn went first. She carried Mellicent to the front of the class and held her up. Mellicent had beautiful yellow glued-on hair, and she was the picture of health. Mr. Travis beamed and wrote an A next to Carolyn's name.

Carolyn started to return to her seat. But before she got there, she stumbled (I swear it was an accident) and Mellicent went flying. We all watched as the unfortunate Mellicent turned in the air, her glorious hair flapping about her, and fell to the floor.

But instead of the usual smacking sound, there was just a gentle cracking as Mellicent shattered into a hundred tiny pieces. There was no yolk, no gore. Nothing at all. Mr. Travis walked over, bent down, and examined the remains of Carolyn's egg.

"Well," he said. "It seems someone tried to get away with blowing out her egg. Would you like to explain this, Miss Pratt?"

Carolyn turned red. She'd been caught. She was an egg-blower. It was a trick none of the rest of us had thought of. We were impressed. But Carolyn had still cheated, and even being the principal's daughter couldn't save her this time.

"I guess that makes Mr. Ford the only responsible parent in the class," Mr. Travis said. He picked up Rupert and shook him, making sure he was still intact. "Good work" he said. "A."

I took Rupert home that afternoon, triumphant. I was a good dad, and I had the grade to prove it. But now that the week was over, I had no idea what to do with my boy. Being a father had been a good experience but I wasn't sure I wanted to spend the next 18 years carting Rupert around and tucking him into the refrigerator every night.

My mother was in the kitchen making a cake. A bowl of eggs sat near her. Sensing my opportunity to be rid of my responsibilities once and for all, I slipped Rupert in next to the plain old eggs and held my breath. When my mother reached into the bowl, I watched as Rupert was lifted out, cracked against the side of a bowl, and mixed into the batter. My mother, too busy reading her recipe, hadn't even noticed his little face as she ended his life. That night, as I ate my piece of chocolate cake, I had pangs of remorse. But that cream cheese frosting was really good, and by the second piece I'd gotten over it.

Now that I'm older and wiser, I watch my gay male friends who have adopted children or acquired them in the usual way, and I think it might be fun to have a kid around. And sometimes when my lesbian friends try to lure me back into fatherhood I'm tempted to give it another try. But then I remember little Rupert, and how good he tasted as a cake, and I think maybe it's not such a good idea after all.

The Nicks Fix

In case you haven't heard, there's a new cure for homosexuality. And you don't have to join one of those annoying ex-gay ministries to take advantage of it. You don't even have to go to a support group or an orientation-reversal therapist. You can experience it in the comfort of your own home. All you have to do is pop a Stevie Nicks CD into your stereo and turn up the volume.

That's right. It's as easy as playing "Stand Back" or "Edge of Seventeen." Why, I imagine you can even dance around and lip-synch while you do it. By the time Stevie and you are done belting out the last "ooh, ooh, ooh," you'll find yourself suddenly wondering what the babes of *Baywatch* are looking like these days.

This remarkable discovery was made by Ronald Anacelteo, a gay man who was recently banned from going anywhere near Nicks after he announced that he knew she could use her magical powers to deliver him from homosexuality. He also revealed that, once cured, it was his firm intention to marry Nicks and have children with her.

You would think this would come as welcome news to the religious right. After all, they've been waging a fierce war in the popular media, taking out full-page newspaper ads announcing that switching from gay to straight is easy as apple pie. Since Nicks is something of a gay icon, having her on their side should be a major coup.

But it's not that simple. See, long before the whole gay-switching thing, the Christians waged a war against the lovely Ms. Nicks. Ever since she announced she was a witch, or at least interested in witchcraft, they've been trying to protect their children from her. When I was but a wee queen, my mother gave me a book describing the horrors of rock music. Stevie had her very own section in this scholarly tome, in which I learned that listening to her music would open wide the doors of my heart to the destructive powers of Satan. "Belladonna is a beautiful but poisonous flower," read one sentence, "and by titling her album with the same name, perhaps Nicks is warning listeners of the potentially deadly content of her songs."

I thought this was interesting, especially as I found it a bit difficult to even make out what Stevie was saying half the time. (When I finally read the liner notes to the albums, I discovered that the words I'd been making up made more sense than the fragmented phrases she was actually warbling.) While the authors of the book claimed lyrics like "sometimes the real color of my skin is my eyes without any shadows" from the song "Nightbird" were thinly veiled odes to the Evil One, I assumed Stevie had just gotten tired of trying to make everything rhyme. Tossing the book aside, I went right on listening to her records.

I even went to a number of her concerts, where I found myself in a sea of girls—and boys—dressed as their goddess, from the top hats down to the perilous high heels. Awash in shawls and diaphanous scarves, they swayed and danced as Stevie sang her heart out. While she most certainly cast a spell on us, if any of the gay men in the audience (and there were many) found themselves suddenly overcome with lust for women, they kept it quiet. As for myself, while I might have wanted to be Stevie, I certainly didn't want to be *with* her.

My mother eventually gave up her battle against Stevie, but the war was not over. For a number of reasons, I found myself attending a Christian college where, among other things, we were encouraged to not listen to rock music and to not be gay. For doing the former, you could expect long lectures from pious fellow students and resident counselors about the dangers of listening to unwholesome lyrics. For doing the latter, you could expect to be summarily expelled and sent back to your parents, who would be duly informed that you were a cocksucker.

Never one to care what others thought, I went right ahead and listened to Stevie, filling my dorm room with her scratchy voice. This did not please my roommate, Paul, a nervous hypochondriac who prided himself on his large collection of ceramic ducks and the brand new Macintosh computer his parents had bought for him. After his first weekend trip home, Paul's overprotective mother phoned to inform me that her son's perpetual colds were being caused by my selfish insistence on keeping at least one window open in the room, and, she implied, by the psychiatric distress of having to hear such pagan thoughts as those expressed by Stevie.

After I hung up on her I spent a happy hour pro-
gramming the music to "Rhiannon," Stevie's famous
ode to the Welsh mare goddess, into Paul's Mac so that
when he turned it on later in the evening it immediately began to play the familiar opening notes. Thinking
that his prized toy had been somehow possessed by the
spirit of Stevie, he became completely unhinged.
Tossing his duck collection into five large boxes, he
hauled them and himself down the hall to the room of
a 45-year-old man who had left his job at a convenience
store to become a freshman Bible major. I enjoyed my
own room for the rest of the semester, and as far as I
know the two of them are still together.

Toward the end of that same year, I also had my first
encounter with the whole ex-gay thing. My friend Jim
decided to make a point by coming out to the dean of students. There was a great deal of fuss and bother, and the
end result was that Jim was sent packing, with the school
declaring he could return only if delivered from the
demon that was causing him to lust after his own kind. I
don't recall exactly why, but Jim agreed to this, and
quickly found himself in a room with the dean, the
school pastor, and several student religious leaders. All of
them laid their hands on him and prayed fervently for
the fey spirit to leave him.

I was not invited to attend this little ceremony, but Jim
says it was quite dramatic. So dramatic that for a brief
time he decided he had, in fact, been freed from the grip
of his gayness. He immediately gave up those things that
reminded him of his "former" life, including a stack of
Stevie CDs, which I quickly snatched up. He even tried
dating, although he chose the girl not because he was

actually attracted to her, but because she had the most fabulous wardrobe in our otherwise fashion-clueless student body. At any rate, both Jim's conversion and his romance were brief affairs, and after a spectacular breakup in which the girl accused him of trying on her favorite pumps, things were back to normal. I even let him have his CDs back.

When I heard about the claims of Mr. Anacelteo, I was immediately taken back to those years when Stevie and the Christians both held prominence in my life. I'd never really wondered about their connection before. But now that they had both come up again in such an obvious way, I saw that they had indeed been parallel influences on my development as a queer man.

How many gay boys, I wonder, sit in their dorm rooms listening to "Beauty and the Beast" or "Two Kinds of Love" and dream of the days when they will be able to love another man the way Stevie's characters love theirs? How many teenage queers attend her concerts and watch her face as she sings, knowing she's singing just to them?

Anyone who has seen Nicks in concert knows she has an almost inexplicable attraction. I've been to Fleetwood Mac concerts where the majority of the attendees were there for one reason: to see Stevie. During the songs sung by Christine McVie or Lindsey Buckingham they clap politely; when Stevie takes the stage they go wild. Watching the faces of Stevie's bandmates, you can tell they wonder what she has that they don't. I don't know what it is either, but it's magic of the oddest kind.

While many of Stevie's legions are women, her gay male fans are among her strongest. For proof, you need only look at the annual Night of a Thousand Stevies party, where throngs of men dressed as Ms. Nicks come together in New York's Jackie 60 club to worship her. It is nothing short of a religious experience. If young gay men are looking for a patron goddess, they need look no further than the wild-haired siren standing before them in platform boots and chain mail headdress. While Mr. Anacelteo and the Christians may hope her touch removes what he sees as a curse, the rest of us go to her for a blessing.

Welcome to the Real World

When MTV first announced plans for its true-life drama *The Real World* several years ago, I thought it was a good idea. After all, America is fascinated by things like *Cops* and *Rescue 911*. Personally, I'm hooked on *Trauma: Life in the E.R.*, where they simply film a different hospital emergency room each week. I don't know why, but I can't help watching.

I suppose I like these shows because I like to see other people do the same stupid things I do. People are all pretty much the same, and knowing this, *The Real World* seemed like a great idea. Stick seven strangers in a house and watch it blow up. And of course it always did: shouting, belligerence, sleeping around, and drama.

But despite a few memorable moments, the show has never offered anything truly interesting. Primarily, I think, this is because there have never been any good queer characters. Yes, there was Norman on the first season, but he was about as interesting as watching Senate debates on CNN. And there were a couple of dykes scattered throughout the other seasons, but they were generally weepy and apologetic, as though someone had told them to keep it low-key or face deportment to

Nickelodeon. What we were left with was a group of straight kids and their lives. And, let's face it, few things are as boring as the daily schedules of heterosexual twentysomethings laid out in agonizing detail.

What very few people know, until now, is that there was an all-gay season of the show. The producers were thrilled with the results, but MTV executives, worried their increasingly conservative viewership wouldn't tune in to watch the lives of a bunch of fags, decided to bury the tapes deep inside the same vault in which they've hidden Martha Quinn. Like some kind of forgotten Cerberus, she sits guarding the unseen tapes from curiosity seekers while waiting for the '80s nostalgia wave to put her back in demand.

Thankfully, one brave soul did manage to get past Martha. After slipping her a sleeping-pill–laced Diet Fresca, our stalwart hero scoured the vault and returned with bounty in hand. Through a circuitous network, the tapes made their way to me. Now, for the first time, I am presenting a blow-by-blow summary of the lost season of *The Real World*.

Imagine, if you will, a lovely restored Victorian in San Francisco, Castro-adjacent with a hot tub and rooftop garden. Into this paradise come seven gay men. They are Geoff (32, an underwriter), Stephen (25, a bartender), Richard (23, a graphic designer), Timothy (29, an actor), Phillip (30, a lawyer), Matthew (age unknown, mysterious employment), and Chad (20, a frat boy).

EPISODE 1: The cast arrives at its new home. Finding that there is only one private room, they each make a case for getting their own space. Timothy wins when it is revealed that he has a habit of reciting lines from *Valley of the Dolls* forcefully in his sleep. The others pair up by comparing favorite aromatherapy scents and mixing and matching to create a perfect blend. They celebrate their first night together with a mescalun salad, penne with goat cheese and sun-dried tomatoes, and a perky zinfandel. The first stirrings of trouble arise when Richard and Phillip disagree over whether to serve the cheesecake with the raspberry coulis on the side or on top.

EPISODE 2: After one week of sleeping in the same room with Matthew, Richard announces that he can't possibly stand one more night of dirty Calvin Klein underwear strewn all over the floor. He moves into Geoff's room and Phillip, who thinks Geoff's obsession with ironing borders on a mental disorder, moves in with Matthew. Because Matthew and Phillip have the same waist size, they are able to share clothing. When Phillip discovers he has crabs, the exact nature of Matthew's employment is revealed as being of the sex-for-pay variety.

EPISODE 3: Geoff uses the last of Stephen's styling gel, and an ugly scene ensues. Forced to go to work with bad hair, Stephen is surly to a regular customer and fired on the spot. To exact revenge, Stephen returns to the house and smashes Geoff's prized copy of the impossible-to-find Julie Andrews *Live in Japan* album. Meanwhile, Chad overhears a phone call in which Timothy mocks his wearing of corduroy pants. He flees the house in tears to search for a more becoming wardrobe.

EPISODE 4: When Richard's parents make an unexpected visit, the entire house must be de-gayed for their arrival, throwing things into complete chaos as hiding places for the Billy and Carlos dolls, Falcon videos, and stray issues of *Honcho* must be found. The roommates are forced to act like straight men for a few days. All goes well at first, but their cover is blown when, while feigning enthusiasm for beer and Monday Night Football, a tipsy Geoff leans over to Richard's father and says, "Man, I'd like to get my hands on that tight end, wouldn't you?"

EPISODE 5: Chad secretly wonders (in the safety of the confessional) if he might not really be bisexual, as he sort of thinks Linda Evangelista has a nice ass. Geoff and Richard, who have not spoken since Richard's outing, finally have a confrontation in which Geoff screams, "You're here. You're queer. Get used to it!" The other housemates take sides but soon forget which side they support and decide to redecorate the living room in a Hawaiian theme for Stephen's upcoming 26th birthday party. When they can't choose between tikis or torches, the whole plan is scrapped in favor of just going to brunch.

EPISODE 6: Richard, in a fit of pique, sleeps with Timothy's boyfriend while Timothy is away at another failed audition. When Timothy discovers the indiscretion, he invites Richard's ex over for dinner and relates in glorious detail exactly what Richard's mother said when she discovered her son was "a cocksucking, disco-loving, butt goblin." Matthew is caught in the seldom-used upstairs bathroom wearing a Catholic schoolgirl outfit while spanking a client. Fleeing the cameramen, the client falls down the stairs, breaks his leg, and is taken away in an ambulance as shocked neighbors look on.

EPISODE 7: The entire cast is sent to Disneyland for Gay Day and to forget the previous week's tragedy. Wearing matching mouse-ear hats, the boys frolic around the park in a rare moment of camaraderie, cavorting on Mr. Toad's Wild Ride and joking about the well-hung corpses on The Pirates of the Caribbean. Geoff, however, without his afternoon nap, gets testy during the evening and tells Phillip, "If you must sing along during the *Beauty and the Beast* live show, you'd better not try singing Celine Dion's parts, because you're no diva." The rest of the trip is subdued, though Matthew fulfills a lifelong dream by feeling up both Chip and Dale at the Main Street Electrical Parade.

EPISODE 8: Phillip and Stephen, who have been flirting wildly for weeks, finally hook up after a long heart-to-heart about the difficulty of getting a really good tan in San Francisco. But as soon as they get into the hot tub, Stephen realizes Phillip is "penilely challenged" and fakes a herpes outbreak to end the budding relationship. Mortified, Phillip leaves the show. He is replaced by Ryan, a 22-year-old mechanic with chronically grease-stained hands and an amazing chest. Timothy lands a part in a local production of *Hello, Dolly!* but worries that playing straight will typecast him.

EPISODE 9: Matthew, chagrined by the incident with

his client, decides to get out of the call boy business and become a legitimate massage therapist. He joins a gay Sex Addicts Anonymous group, then pisses off the rest of the house by announcing that his Higher Power is Judy Garland and she wants him to throw out all the drugs and liquor in the house. After one too many of his speeches, Ryan slips some Ecstasy into Matthew's bottled water and he snaps out of it. While cleaning out Phillip's dresser to make room for his white T-shirt collection, Ryan finds unsent love letters written to the show's producer. The housemates take turns doing dramatic readings of them on air.

EPISODE 10: Chad, who we find to our surprise is a virgin, decides that his first time will be with Ryan, who is more than happy to oblige. Things take a nasty turn, though, when they can't decide which one will be the top. Geoff mistakenly takes Matthew's Xanax instead of his daily vitamin supplement and spends the rest of the episode insisting he is Bette Davis. Assuming a post-workout Stephen to be Joan Crawford, he attempts to settle once and for all who is the greatest actress through a wrestling competition. The matter remains undecided due to Geoff's falling asleep in the midst of a headlock.

EPISODE 11: Richard has a crisis when his parents announce they are cutting him out of their very substantial will unless he goes straight. He attends a meeting of an ex-gay group where he meets Chris, a former short-stop for a lesbian softball team who tells him to try masturbating to the Victoria's Secret catalog. He tries, but at the next meeting is thrown out when it is discovered he has inserted contraband pages from the International Male circular in between the bra shots. Chad, still suffering from virginity, arranges a date with a man he meets online. Unfortunately, HungJockGuy turns out to be his married 58-year-old high school chemistry teacher.

EPISODE 12: Having more or less survived three months with one another, the housemates decide to hold a blowout of a party. Differences are put aside as the house is turned into a fantasy land of Christmas lights, buffet tables, and gourmet food. In the excitement, no one notices that Ryan has moved out early, taking with him Richard's original Warhol, Timothy's leather jacket, Stephen's Jeff Stryker dildo, Chad's favorite baseball cap, Matthew's little black book, Geoff's American Express card, and the poppers from every bedside table in the house. When the theft is discovered, each man blames the others and exits in a huff, leaving the mess for the maid to clean up.

Sticker Shock

One afternoon a few weeks ago, my roommate pulled up to the house in a car that wasn't his.

"What's that?" I asked from my perch on the front steps where the dog and I were sitting.

"It's your new car," he said, tossing me a set of keys.

"I didn't buy a car," I said. I looked suspiciously at the dog. Just a few days before there had been in the mail an offer for a platinum Visa card in his name, so I had reason to be wary. But he just looked at the car with interest and kept quiet.

"I got a great deal on it at the garage where I have my car fixed," my roommate explained. "You need a car, and I figured this was a good way to pay you back for when I was out of work and couldn't pay rent."

And just like that, I became a car owner. I'm still not sure it's a good idea. I've always been content to walk wherever I want to go. In fact, my choices of living situations have always been heavily weighted toward whether I can easily get to grocery stores, video stores, and restaurants on foot. When I got the dog, I added parks to the list. Beyond those four basic things, I don't really need to go anywhere. And if some rare occasion calls for transport, I can always find someone to take me.

It's not that I don't like cars. I do. But I don't like driving them; I like riding in them. Driving involves responsibility, paying attention to other drivers, and knowing where you're going. Riding involves having control over the radio, staring out the window at interesting things, and being able to eat with both hands while staying on the road. If someone else will drive, I'm happy to go along, especially if I can open the window and stick my head out. But I don't enjoy being behind the wheel.

"What do you mean you don't like to drive?" my friend Katherine said when I told her about the new car and how I was reluctant to take it anywhere. Katherine adores driving. She lives in New York, where you can have absolutely everything delivered, and she still has a car she uses every day.

"Think about it," I said patiently, having gone over and over this particular topic many times in my head. "There are ten billion things that can go wrong. I could accidentally go from drive to reverse and the car would drop its innards all over the highway. The ventilation system could make the windshield fog up and I'd cross into oncoming traffic while trying to wipe it off. I might skid off a bridge and drown because the electrical system shorted out and I couldn't open the power windows."

"Those things are not going to happen," Katherine said with the reasonable air of someone who has been driving for years.

"I might have to make a left turn," I tried helplessly.

"Just get in the damn car," she ordered.

As it turned out, before I could actually get into the car and take it anywhere, I had to register and insure it. This involved standing in 63 different lines and filling out 500 forms, none of which I did correctly. I didn't know what the exact mileage was on the odometer. I couldn't trace the succession of owners back to the day the car rolled off the assembly line. I drew a blank when the insurance salesman asked if I wanted blanket collision coverage or a per-item deductible based on standard industry scales.

Yet somehow I managed to get through it all, and ended up with a car that was registered, insured, and inspected. Secretly I'd hoped the inspector would find something—perhaps a giant hole in a crucial part of the exhaust system—that would render the car unfit, saving me from actually having to drive it. That was not to be, however, and my car turned out to be a perfect specimen of automotive design.

But before I could actually consider the process finished, there was one final decision to be made.

"What kind of sticker are you going to put on the bumper?" my friend Diane asked as we stood looking at my newly insured and approved conveyance.

"Sticker?" I said.

"Sure," she said. "You need a sticker. It's your statement about who you are. Otherwise it's just a car."

Suddenly, the whole notion of car ownership took on an entirely new dimension. Before, I'd thought of it as something to get around in if need be. But now it was an accessory. I had a reason to be interested.

"You mean people actually pay attention to what kind of sticker you have?" I asked.

"Oh, definitely," she said. "I've turned down dates with people just because they had stickers that said MEAN PEOPLE SUCK. I figure if they're willing to put something that lame on their car, it won't be long before I'm getting found-object earrings as a birthday present. Who needs it?"

I started to think. I knew I wanted a gay-themed sticker. The times I'd been riding around in unfamiliar territory while traveling, seeing a pink triangle or other identifying sticker on another car had always been reassuring. So off we went to the local gay bookstore, where I discovered a dizzying array of stickers, all in rainbow colors.

"How about this flag?" I suggested. "It's simple and to the point."

Diane scoffed. "That is so last year," she said. She picked up a rainbow peace sign. "How about this? Two messages in one."

"I don't think so," I said. "It's too Grateful Dead."

I wanted to find just the right sticker—one that would make a comment about some part of gay culture I have an interest in. We looked at rainbow triangles, rainbow Mars symbols, and rainbow cowboy boots. We considered and rejected rainbow-tinted stickers shaped like the Commonwealth of Massachusetts, a dog paw, and the word *butch*.

I was just about to give up and settle for last year's rainbow flag when I unearthed a rainbow sticker shaped like a bear. Having something of an affinity for hairy men, I thought it would be nice to let them know an admirer was driving along in front of them.

I put the rainbow bear on my rear bumper, where it looked very proud indeed next to the Southern New England AAA sticker. I had visions of someday needing a tow and happily discovering the studly tow truck driver, clued in by my rainbow bear sticker, was playing on my team.

I finally began to drive the car around, tentatively at first. I was a little shaky after more than a decade of being a simple pedestrian. But after a couple of days when nothing really awful happened, I started to loosen up. It was kind of nice to be able to go to the grocery store whenever I wanted and to not have to carry the laundry down the street. Best of all, I started to notice all of the rainbow stickers affixed to bumpers and rear windows as I drove around. It was great to see family on the road, and I imagined people noticing my rainbow bear and nodding in solidarity. But what I was really waiting for was the chance to use it as date bait.

Then one day, when I drove the dog to the park for his evening swim, a man who was parked near me in a pick-up stuck his head out of his window. "Hey," he said. "Nice sticker."

Here we go, I thought excitedly, noting his outdoorsy look and flannel shirt. *It's working*.

"It's great to see that," he said, smiling. "Makes me feel right at home."

I noted his hairy forearm where it rested along the window's edge. I tried to get a closer look at his open shirt to see just how bear-like he really was.

"Well," I said, taking the plunge. "Most guys are into that smooth look. But that just leaves more hairy men for the rest of us."

He gave me a weird look. "Hairy guys?" he said.

"Yeah," I answered. "You know, bears. Hair. Bears."

"Oh," he said after a moment. He sounded disappointed. "I get it now. Sorry. I thought it stood for gay guys from Maine. I'm visiting from Bangor, and I thought you might be from around there too."

With that, he rolled up his window and left, before I could even offer to pack up my things and move farther north with him. Dejected, I turned to let the dog out of the car.

But I couldn't. In my excitement, I'd shut the door and left the keys inside.

When You Wish
Upon a Star

The end of a year is always a little depressing for me. I'm a pop culture junkie and, inevitably, as December rolls around, I start seeing reports about all of the celebrities who have died during the previous 12 months. I've generally noted each death throughout the year, but run together collectively they become unsettling. As clip after clip flashes on the screen showing the most memorable contributions of each of the deceased, I feel a whole row of doors slamming shut at once.

The problem is that we're running out of stars. I mean *real* stars, people like Bette Davis and Marlene Dietrich and Cary Grant. Stars who electrified audiences and made Hollywood seem like the most magical place on earth. As each luminary twinkles out, life becomes the tiniest bit less exciting.

Perhaps this is a form of depression peculiar to gay men. After all, we are the societal custodians of all things fabulous and artificial, right? We embrace the love stories and melodramas of the silver screen with open arms, finding in the lives of our stars the lives we maybe wish we had ourselves. Even the launching of our modern gay rights movement is believed to in no small way have been influenced by the untimely death of one of our greatest film icons, Judy Garland. Perhaps seeing her inability to stay in the world made us decide to change things.

All right, so maybe pining after dead celebrities is a little shallow. There are, of course, more important things to worry about. But I can't help feeling the death of true stardom is something to be lamented, particularly by gay culture. Many of us, long before we knew why we were different from the other kids, found kinship with the faces we saw on the screen, be it movie or television. Something about those faces drew us in and made us feel more comfortable about ourselves.

I admit that I never understood the fuss over *The Wizard of Oz*, but that's probably because I read the book as a kid and liked it better than the movie. I do, however, distinctly remember the first time I saw Bette Davis. The tiny video store in our country town had a small shelf of classics, most of which I'd never heard of. But we had been discussing Lillian Hellman in school, and when I saw that her play *The Little Foxes* had been made into a film, I decided to check it out.

If I wasn't gay before that moment, then that's certainly what did it. Watching Bette Davis tear through Hellman's story of a bitter woman wreaking havoc on everyone around her, I could only sit wide-eyed. I watched every sneer of Davis's lips, every arch of her eyebrows. I watched the scene where she looks at her husband, close to death from a heart condition, and says, cold as ice, "I hope you die, Horace. I hope you die *real* soon," over and over. I couldn't believe someone could be so horrible and so enchanting all at once.

I had, as it turns out, seen Bette before, in Disney's

Return From Witch Mountain when I was ten. But that
was a different Bette, a Bette worn down by a changing
Hollywood system that eschewed plot and sparkling dialogue for UFOs and talking cats. I hadn't then been old
enough to appreciate that she was doing the best she
could with what she'd been given.

But now I took to her as if I'd stumbled upon an oasis
after a walk through the desert. For the next week or so,
I watched Bette every night, wearing out the store's mea-
ger collection. *Hush…Hush, Sweet Charlotte. Now,
Voyager. Dark Victory. Pocketful of Miracles. Old Maid.
Jezebel. The Letter.* My parents, probably pleased that I
had stopped bringing home horror films, watched in
bemused silence as I sat, transfixed, and watched the dra-
mas unfold. Even more peculiar was how, after the films
were done, I remembered lines of dialogue and looked
for opportunities to use them in real life. It was as if some
hitherto untapped part of my brain had been opened,
and its voice sounded eerily like Bette in *All About Eve*.

For a long time I thought I was the only one who had
this peculiar affliction. Then, shortly after I moved to
New York, a friend took me to a screening of *What Ever
Happened to Baby Jane?* at the now-defunct Theater 80, a
revival house that showed nothing but classics. The place
was filled to capacity with gay men. The curtains parted
and the film began, and all around me I heard the script
being read, as half of the audience played the Joan
Crawford role, speaking her lines to perfection, while the
other half took up the Bette Davis part, complete with
mannerisms. I knew at that moment that I had found my
people. No, we weren't changing the world that night,
but we had a great time, and it became an annual event

for my friends and me—sort of the gay version of going to a *Messiah* sing-along at holiday time.

That experience is something we don't get much of anymore in this era of impersonal multiplexes and films noted more for their budgets than for their stories. The sad fact is, we just don't have any stars to replace Bette and Joan. None of Hollywood's current elite has real style. Tom Hanks may be affable, but I doubt he makes many of us fantasize about being stranded on a desert island with him the way Rock Hudson did. And while Garbo said as much by not speaking as most actresses did in their scene-chewing monologues, the best that today's hot actresses like Demi Moore and Meg Ryan can do is try not to put us to sleep.

One of the things I am most proud of from the past year or two is that I did not see James Cameron's *Titanic*. As far as I'm concerned, this piece of dreck is the ultimate example of how dim Hollywood's star has become. Leonardo DiCaprio as a romantic hero? Kate Winslet as the heroine who needs to be taken down a few rungs so she sees how the other half lives? Please. Clark Gable and Claudette Colbert's mismatched lovers fighting across a screen of strung-up laundry beats out this floundering version any day, and without a billion dollars worth of special effects. The 13-year-olds mooning over Leonardo and Kate when they've never seen *Casablanca* or *The Philadelphia Story* have no idea how cheated they really are.

But gay men know what we're missing. We see Hollywood's star doing a slow fade to black, and we know it signals an end to something we'll almost certainly never see again. We might quote the occasional line from a new movie, but we know in our hearts that Arnold muttering "I'll be back" will never carry the same weight as "Did you hear, Blanche? We've got *rats* in the cellar."

Indeed, those of us searching for new icons to replace the ones we've lost are hard pressed to find anything worthy of adoration. We gave Madonna a chance, but she turned out to be more interested in self-promotion than in doing anything truly interesting. In 40 years, when we turn on the television and hear that she's passed, we might feel some nostalgic pangs as we recall the first time we heard "Like a Virgin," but will we really be crushed? And while I will be the first to say that staring at Ben Affleck for a few hours is a wonderful way to pass the time, I don't think there will be a rush of queer moviegoers lining up to see the rerelease of *Armageddon* in 2048 because they recall it fondly as the movie that made them long to be in love.

When Lucille Ball died I cried a little. When Myrna Loy died I cried a lot. And yes, I felt a little silly doing it. I didn't know these women. They didn't know me. But they gave me something very special over the years. They made me laugh. They created characters and played out stories that I connected with. They helped me dream. And I connected to other people who also loved them. No, it's not the same as taking someone's hand at Stonewall and standing up for gay rights. It's not the same as marching with thousands of other gay women and men to demand funding for AIDS research. But it was something very real, something uniquely queer, and I treasure it.

I hope young gay people will find their own stars.

Maybe they don't need them in the way that people my age and older did. Maybe they don't feel the need to escape into worlds where things are a little more interesting, a little more romantic, a little more glamorous. But I hope they do. I hope they find their own icons and their own common reference points, the lines from movies that they repeat over and over and still find funny or moving or empowering. I hope that one day they can all sit in a darkened theater, the kind with a really big screen and velvet curtains that sweep the floor, holding hands with their dates and watching one of their favorite movies play while they recite all the lines together and laugh until it hurts.

Growing Pains

I am a grown-up. I know this because this morning for breakfast I ate half a bag of Reese's miniature peanut butter cups. If I were a child, someone would have stopped me.

But I don't always feel like a grown-up. In fact, most of the time I sit around waiting for someone to tell me what to do next, as if the bell ending recess rang but I can't remember where my classroom is. I keep hoping a hall monitor will happen along and point me in the right direction. The peanut butter cups were clearly an act of rebellion.

Some people take to the whole grown-up thing with ease. They get jobs and plan for their futures. They have cocktails with friends, take vacations, and follow the financial news. These people frighten me. Sometimes I sit on the subway and look at them with their briefcases, neat haircuts, and stylish clothes, wondering how they got that way. Clearly we all started out on the same road. But at some point they took the exit leading to adulthood. I, apparently, was busy trying to find a really good station on the radio and missed my turn.

It's not that I don't do the requisite adult things. I pay

my bills every month. I have a credit card. I have a car. But sometimes I still find myself in front of the television thinking, *You really should turn that off and go outside to play.* And on more than one occasion I have had to remind myself that no one is forcing me to get up at six every morning, and that I really could grab another couple of hours if I wanted to. But I do it anyway, urged on by some kind of groundless fear that if I continue to sleep someone is sure to give me hell for it.

When my parents were the age I am now, they had a house and three children. I have a rented apartment and a dog, but it's hardly the same. For one, the dog's toys cost less, and he'll never demand to be taken to a Spice Girls concert because all his friends are going and if he doesn't they'll say he's not cool.

Sometimes, as I look at myself while shaving, I wonder if my father used to stand in front of the mirror in the morning in the same way and wait for the moment when everyone would figure out that underneath the suit and tie he wore to work he was really still 13 years old. Because that's what I do. Not that I own a suit or tie or have a real job. I sit at home in my boxer shorts and write. But I still worry that one day there will be a knock on the door and some official-looking person will announce in a loud voice that the jig is up and I have to go back to junior high with the other kids.

When I was in my early teens, I used to look at my sisters' college friends and think they were very grown-up. Then, when I was in college, I looked at people who had graduated and started their lives and thought that they were very grown-up. A few years later, having graduated myself and toiling in a real job, I started getting suspicious.

The grown-ups were getting older and older, and I was always five or six years behind them. The height of the adulthood bar kept rising, and more and more it looked as if I would never clear it.

Finally I gave up. I admitted to myself that I was never going to be one of those truly grown-up people who knows what he's doing. And that's OK. That's why the world has people like Dan Rather and Oprah. They figure it all out and break it to the rest of us in terms we can understand. Thanks to them, I don't need to be able to talk about health plans and politics with any sense of assuredness. I can just sit around playing with blocks until Oprah and Dan fill me in.

Sometimes I'm fine, and for a while I go around feeling like I can cope. I'll be wheeling my cart through the grocery store, throwing things into it, and I'll realize I can do this any time I feel like it. Or I'll have the sudden thought that I can just get in my car and drive somewhere without permission. *Why*, I think excitedly, *I could buy a plane ticket to Tibet or paint my bedroom some exotic color, and no one could say anything about it*. At those moments, being grown-up seems almost worth it.

But most of the time it just freaks me out. Worse, I fear that others are suffering from the same condition and not letting on. As a kid, I looked at the adults around me and assumed they knew what they were doing; doctors knew what was best for my health; the people flying the airplane could handle it; and people in charge of the government were capable and worthy individuals. After all, they were grown-ups. Grown-ups could do anything, and someday I would be just like them.

Now someday has come, and if the other adults are

anything like me, we're in big trouble. This frightens me. When I go to the doctor I don't look at his framed degrees from Harvard and feel reassured. I study his face as he talks, and conclude that he has no idea what he's doing and is making up all those big words to save face. When I sit in an airplane during takeoff, I imagine the pilot up front staring at the switches on his instrument panel, trying to remember what does what and hoping his copilot was more awake during class than he was. As for the government, let's just say I do not watch our elected leaders on television and feel any sense of pride or confidence. After all, people like me elected them, and what the hell do we know?

A couple of months back I spoke to a group of third-graders at a local elementary school about what it's like being a writer. During the question-and-answer period, I looked around at the shiny faces staring at me, at the hands waving frantically in the air as they waited to be called on. Choosing one, I asked an eager little girl what she wanted to know.

"How old are you?" she asked. The other hands went down, as if every one of the kids wanted to know the same thing.

"I'm 30," I answered, having just endured that birthday.

All around me, eyes went wide. The children gawked as if I were a newly discovered relic pulled from the desert sands of Arizona or something.

"That's so old," said one boy.

"You're older than my mom," added another, disbelieving.

Things went on in this way for some time. The children wanted to know how someone as clearly aged as I was could write books, let alone walk to their school without the aid of a cane.

I, of course, was looking at them and wondering what I could possibly say that would ever be of any use to them. Tucked into one of their tiny chairs, I didn't feel much older than they were. Yet there they were, asking me for advice and answers. I knew that if I told them to stand on their heads, they'd probably all do it, simply because I was taller than they were. I wanted to say, "Don't you understand? I don't know anything."

When I left that day, the teacher accompanied me to the doors of the school. "You should never tell them how old you are," she said consolingly. "It's like throwing raw meat to coyotes. I just tell them I knew God when he was a boy. That shuts them up. Except for the ones who want to know if he was a good kickball player."

But I know how those kids feel. They look at me and wonder what their lives will be like a billion years later when they too are 30. I'm sure they have all kinds of plans about being models and football stars and of having stylish clothes, nice cars, and big houses. Next time, I'll tell them the truth.

"You still won't know what you want to be when you grow up," I'll say. "You'll wonder why everyone else has great jobs and wonderful relationships and dogs who sleep on the floor, because in all likelihood you won't have won that Oscar, your significant other really won't be that good in bed, and your dog will throw up on your shoes every chance it gets. You might luck out and make a lot of money, but chances are you'll be eating spaghetti and shopping at Wal-Mart while you try to pay off student loans and the credit card bills you racked up when you were 23 and thought it would all take care of itself."

Probably they will just stare at me for a few moments, wondering if I've succumbed to some hideous form of mental illness brought on by advanced age. And then I'll feel bad for ruining their lives.

"OK," I'll tell them gently. "It's not that bad. You can eat peanut butter cups for breakfast." That should give anyone hope.

The Condensed Guide to First Dates

First dates. We've all had them. For some of us, it's all we ever have. But whether we're first timers or old pros, the prospect of a first date is both thrilling and nauseating. Let's face it: A first date is nothing but a test drive. If everything feels right, there might be a sale. But if something goes awry, it's on to the next model in the showroom.

The key to a successful first date is romance. *What's that? Who says romance is dead?* OK, well, you're right. I did just last week. But I was in a really bad mood. The truth is, there's no reason why gay men can't be as sickeningly sweet as the rest of the world when it comes to romance. In fact, we're predisposed to be better at it because we know the difference between a tacky Whitman's sampler and real Godiva. Plus, we've spent years watching old movies and weeping over the love stories. Being able to put that knowledge to good use is what sets us apart from the animals. And from straight men.

For some of us, romance comes easily. For others it's a learned art. So if you have your eye on Mr. Right, this is the time to get it together. And even if you don't have a sweetie pie in mind to play kissy-face with at the moment, listen up. Someday you will, and you'll want to know what to do to make him fall in love with you and stick around for the rest of your life. That means making sure your first date together is unforgettable. To help you, I've provided a step-by-step guide to romancing your would-be prince.

Step 1: Getting His Attention

You've found the man you want. You know he's The One. That's a great start. But before you start planning the wedding, you have to get him to say yes to a first date. You could just ask him, but anyone can do that. You want to make sure he knows you mean business. The true romantic understands the best way to make a man take notice is through bribery disguised as thoughtfulness. Accompany your request with some little token of affection. If he's open to being romanced, your intended will love it. If he's not, he'll probably still say yes just so he can keep the gift and not feel guilty. Romantic: flowers, love notes, chocolates. Not Romantic: subpoenas, suicide threats, cash.

Step 2: Setting the Mood

Once you've convinced your dream guy to join you for a romantic get-together, it's crucial to pick the perfect activity for your first encounter. You want to create a mood that is casual yet ripe with possibilities. The right romantic date will flower into something incredible, while a botched attempt will end with you alone, watching porn videos and jerking off into your sock. So plan carefully. Remember, this is the date you'll look back on

30 years from now as the one that started it all. Romantic: dinner at your favorite intimate restaurant, a walk along the beach talking about your dreams, a symphony concert under the stars. Not Romantic: dinner at any restaurant where the food comes packaged with a toy, a walk along the beach talking about your ex, a Mormon Tabernacle Choir concert.

Step 3: Using Your Mouth

Conversation is crucial to romance. More than one reluctant lover has been persuaded to give it up by a smooth-talking paramour, and a couple of well-chosen words whispered breathlessly into an ear can mean the difference between hours of fun and a quick good-bye. "I want to make love to you for the rest of the night," said at the right time, can work wonders. So can, "How about tying me to the bed and smacking my ass with that belt?" To determine the best lines for your particular situation, you must know your audience, but the general principle is the same. The following suggestions should get you started. Romantic: "I could look into your eyes forever," "I can't wait to wake up in your arms tomorrow morning," "I don't think I've ever wanted to undress someone this much." Not Romantic: "I think my infection has cleared up," "We only have 20 minutes until my lover/parents/Mother Superior come home," "I'm so glad you aren't one of those guys who only likes big dicks."

Step 4: Getting It On

You've gotten him to notice you, gotten him home, and gotten him into bed. (No, not every first date ends up in the sack. In fact, some people think waiting a couple of dates is the romantic thing to do. But while they're waiting, the rest of us are ready for action.) You might think it's OK to toss romance out the window since your date is already in the bag, so to speak. But no. This is the time to really play it up, especially if you want him to come back. He can get a good hard fuck anywhere; you need to show him you have even more to offer. When it's time for action, put your imagination in high gear and give him a night he'll never forget. Even if you don't end up together forever, he'll compare all the rest to you. Romantic: running an ice cube over his skin and following it with your tongue, asking him to tell you his fantasy and then giving it to him, massaging his back for an hour before you even touch his dick. Not Romantic: asking him to move over a little because the camera isn't getting everything, putting a towel underneath his ass to protect your Laura Ashley sheets "just in case," falling asleep before he comes.

Step 5: Keeping Him Around

Getting a guy for a night may be enough for some men, but the hopeless romantic is looking for a full-time position. If you're successful, you may be rewarded with a guy who thinks you're the sweetest man who ever lived. But before you get to keep the title, you have to get him to come back. Whether he does will have a lot to do with how you treat him the morning after. If you want to see him again, make sure you send him off wanting more. Romantic: waking him with a kiss, bringing him breakfast in bed, taking a shower with him. Not Romantic: waking him by sitting on his face, giving him bus fare and directions to the nearest stop, telling him not to use the blue toothbrush because it's your boyfriend's.

High Times

You know you've lived a sheltered life when a presidential candidate has done more drugs than you have.

I was watching CNN the other night and they were interviewing Democratic presidential hopeful Bill Bradley. The issue about Republican candidate George W. Bush's alleged past drug use came up, and in the course of the discussion Bradley was asked if he'd ever smoked pot.

"On several occasions," Bradley answered without hesitation.

"And did you inhale?" joked the questioner, referring to Bill Clinton's infamous claim about having smoked pot without actually smoking pot.

"I did indeed," said Bradley.

Well, he's one up on me. I've never smoked pot. Well, once I tried, but I did it all wrong and ended up wheezing a lot. Besides, I hated the smell, and I never tried again. In fact, I've never done any drugs of any kind. No Ecstasy. No coke. Not even poppers, which technically aren't a drug but which gay men seem to go wild for.

Now, please don't think I'm taking the moral high road here. I haven't steered clear of altering my consciousness through chemicals for any particularly pious reasons. It's just that I'm bad enough without them. I don't even take cold medicine unless I'm absolutely dying and convinced that my nasal passages are closing up for good. And even then I only take half the recommended dose, because it's sure to knock me out for hours and leave me nauseous afterward. When I had to have my wisdom teeth out, the doctor gave me a prescription for Tylenol with codeine. I took one and woke up three days later convinced I was in a Turkish prison.

The problem is that my body doesn't handle stimulation very well. Things that give other people mild buzzes, like caffeine or sugar, send me into overdrive. A couple of years ago I decided I needed to start drinking coffee because that's what writers do. Besides, I liked the idea of having a coffee maker and a little machine to grind the beans. So I bought them and launched myself headlong into the exciting world of java. I trotted over to a coffee store, thrilled that such a thing could even exist, and got myself a pound of some exotically named beans. Then I ground them up, set the machine to perking, and waited.

The first cup was sort of OK. It woke me up, and I felt a warm glow as I sat in front of my computer drinking it. When it was done, I poured myself another. By 10 o'clock in the morning I had consumed six cups because I didn't want to waste what I'd made, Kenyan blue mountain coffee beans costing what they do. My whole body was trembling, and I found myself reading the same paragraph over and over and over, unable to make any sense of it and desperately trying to remember if *chrysanthemum* was really even a word. Finally I laid down on the floor and stared at the ceiling, wondering if my heart was going to leap out of my chest. That was my last experience with the coffee machine. The next day I packed it up and gave it to a friend whose years of coffee drinking had left her immune to anything weaker than 100% black Columbian roast injected directly into her veins. I went back to Ovaltine, and gladly.

While the physical issue is one thing, I admit that my inexperience with drugs is also at least partly because I fear losing control. This I blame on Angeline Kennedy. Angeline was my school's resident pothead. She and I were friends, and she made it her mission to get me high. While outwardly I protested, secretly I wanted her to make good on her threat because it seemed like such a bad boy thing to do. But I was also convinced that if I touched a joint someone would surely get me for it, probably God.

One day Angeline arrived at lunch with a smile on her face and a small bag in her hand. It was, she said, marijuana. The real thing. I looked at it with a rapidly growing sense of alarm and wonder, and asked what she was going to do with it. She opened the bag, took a pinch of the green leaves, and proceeded to sprinkle them over the little carton of strawberry ice cream that was a part of our lunch that day.

"Dig in," she said, grinning.

I took a spoonful of the pot-covered ice cream and tasted it. Pot is not the culinary equivalent of chocolate sprinkles, but I figured that since I'd stuck my toe in the water I might as well go in all the way. I quickly ate the rest of it and put the dish down.

"I don't feel anything," I said to Angeline.

"Don't worry," she said. "It takes a while."

As it happened, that afternoon my mother and I were driving to my sister's house, which was about five hours away. She picked me up at school right after lunch. As I got into the car, I wondered if she could tell I was high. Because I was sure that I must be high. After all, I'd eaten pot. I settled nervously into my seat and tried to remember all the signs of drug use we'd learned about in health class. I wanted to be able to hide them from my mother. I kept trying to look at my eyes in the rearview mirror to see if they were bloodshot, and I tried not to fidget. If my mother noticed, she didn't say anything.

For the entire five-hour trip I debated whether or not I was high. I didn't really feel any different, but I knew that I must be under some kind of influence. After all, I'd ingested real live marijuana. I even tried being more high than I seemed to be, squinting my eyes and giggling a little. But I just felt stupid and eventually I settled into a morose silence, trying to console myself with the thought that I was in a car with my mother and I was stoned. Very movie-of-the-week. Very after-school special. I imagined myself getting high on a regular basis, hiding the pot from my mother inside a hollowed-out Bible or something. My grades would slip, and I would start to have friends of dubious reputation. It would all be very wicked, and when it was over I would be a different person, edgier and streetwise like the girls in the novels I sometimes got from our church library who ran away from home, became hookers, and had to be rescued from foulmouthed pimps by their dedicated and surprisingly attractive youth group leaders.

All weekend I remained in my newfound druggie

persona. I sat on the couch, watching my sister and my mother and thinking, *They have no idea that I use*. If they asked me questions, I lied just for the practice. I knew it would come in handy later on. By the time we returned home on Sunday night, I was ready for the big time. On Monday when I saw Angeline, I asked her when she could score for me again.

"That wasn't pot," she said, laughing. "It was oregano. I was just fooling with you."

I've been getting high on oregano ever since.

The sad truth is, I wouldn't know a real drug experience from the one I convinced myself I was having, so why bother? Plus, I worry that the very second my consciousness is altered the house will catch fire from some freak accident and I won't be coherent enough to get the dog out. I realize this fear is the vestigial remains of good old Baptist guilt, but it's there nonetheless. I just know that if I were to snort cocaine, it would inevitably come from a bag that had been cut with rat poison and my brain would explode on the spot. Or if I were to take acid (oddly the only drug that actually appeals to me, probably because I imagine that being on it would be a lot like watching Disney's *Fantasia*) I would end up believing I could fly and find myself climbing utility poles to prove it.

Honestly, I don't think I've missed anything by not playing with drugs. I have many friends who have done more than enough for both of us, and they assure me that, while sometimes amusing, overall drugs are nothing to write home about. But when a presidential candidate, of all people, has done more than you have, it makes you wonder if maybe you haven't been just a little too uptight.

Besides, I don't want anyone to think I actually listened to
Nancy Reagan in the '80s and agreed with her.

The problem is that it's too late to start now.
Experimenting with drugs at 22 is sort of hip and expected, like announcing that you're a communist for a week
or two, but at 30-something it's like buying a red convertible and trading in your perfectly wonderful
boyfriend for a moody French underwear model. It just
means you're trying too hard. Instead, I have accepted
that I am not the thrill-seeking kind when it comes to
that kind of thing. I'll leave the coke and the Ecstasy and
even the coffee to other people. I have the memories of
my oregano weekend to get me by when I need to go
back to my wild days. And if I want to relive them, all I
have to do is eat one too many chocolate bars, wash them
down with some Mountain Dew, and within minutes
I'm flying high.

Test of Faith

Probably the most dramatic story to emerge from the 1999 shooting rampage at Columbine High School in Littleton, Colorado, is that of Cassie Bernall. Cassie became a modern-day martyr when, within hours of her death in the school library, a story began to circulate that she was shot at point-blank range after the two boys who initiated the killing spree asked her if she was a Christian and she answered that she was. It didn't take long for an eager press to pounce on the story and for Christian groups around the country to turn Cassie into a role model for young people everywhere.

The response to this story was overwhelming. It seemed that no report about the tragedy at Littleton was complete without a mention of Cassie's willingness to die for her faith. Pictures of her beautiful smiling face appeared everywhere, and across the country young people moved by her story turned to their churches and youth groups in record numbers. It is not unreasonable to say that what happened at Columbine High School, and particularly to Bernall, launched a religious revival among the teenage set.

It also launched a renewed discussion about the issue

of religious oppression in America. Well, maybe not a discussion exactly. More like a medium-size hysteria on the part of right wing religious zealots. Suddenly, in their minds, the Columbine attack became an attack on religion, specifically Christianity. From church pulpits to the halls of Congress, concerned voices called for a return to "traditional Christian values" that would teach children not to kill one another, as well as increased awareness of the plight of oppressed Christians throughout the land.

I always think it's interesting when Christian people talk about being persecuted. One day many years ago, my Baptist Sunday school teacher told us we were going to pretend to be a group of early Christians. This involved going into a small room in the church and sitting in the dark to approximate the experience of holding worship services in caves to escape persecution by the Romans. We thought this was great fun until we heard the stomping of heavy feet on the stairs outside the room and a moment later the door was shoved open and some of us were dragged, not gently, out into the hallway, where we were placed under arrest and summarily sentenced to death for worshiping the Christian God.

While I have abandoned nearly everything I learned in Sunday school, this is one lesson I have never forgotten. Even though the Roman guards were well-known to me—they were mostly high-school boys whose brothers and sisters were in my class—for a moment I truly believed we were going to be killed, and probably in some gruesome way involving lions, disembowelment, or crucifixion. As I stood in the hallway, I remember wondering if, when asked, I would admit to loving Jesus or instead act as if I'd never heard his name. Thankfully,

I never had to find out. Our teacher, sensing we'd gotten the point, let us trot back upstairs for cookies and juice.

That's about as close to religious persecution as most Christians in the United States ever come. Yet to hear some of them carry on, you'd think they were as endangered as spotted owls. Which brings us back to Littleton, Colorado, and Cassie Bernall. Recently there has been speculation that the story of Bernall's admission of belief, and her death as a result, is not entirely based in fact. A number of things suggest that there wasn't time for her to have had any kind of conversation with her killers at all. It has also been revealed that her intense devotion to church and God was largely a result of her parents forcing her to attend youth group after becoming concerned over her moodiness and rebellious behavior. So who knows how much of her devotion was genuine and how much was an attempt to get mom and dad off her back?

It doesn't really matter, because whatever the truth is, Cassie Bernall has become a poster child for religious martyrdom. Her death touched people in a way that is undeniable. Yet despite my sadness at her death, it's hard for me to feel sorry for the people who are claiming her murder as an example of their own oppression. As Christian fundamentalists blather on about how their rights and the values they stand for are being eroded, they turn a blind eye to the pain they and their own teachings inflict. Cassie Bernall was gunned down by two boys who, among other things, endured almost constant taunting from the same Christian kids whose church families lauded their commitment to Christ at their funerals. Women exercising their right to reproductive choice and the people who assist them are killed with astonishing frequency by zealots claiming to be carrying out God's work. Fred Phelps, with his "God Hates Fags" message, is about as far from the teachings of Jesus Christ as you can possibly get, as are the televangelists who tearfully ask their well-meaning but horribly misguided audiences to part with their hard-earned money in return for vague blessings and promises of eternal reward. Yet they claim they're being threatened with extinction when anyone suggests they might not be all they're cracked up to be.

It's difficult for me to listen to claims of oppression from people who have never really been oppressed. Christianity is the dominant religion of the United States. The Christian God is in our Constitution, in our Pledge of Allegiance, and even on our money. Despite the separation of church and state, political candidates regularly use their religious views as platforms. The Christian Coalition is one of the most aggressive political groups in the world. Lawmakers bowing to pressure from Christian constituencies are trying to get prayer back in schools at the same time that they're trying to make the practices of other religions illegal. But somehow these same people are convinced they feel the pinch of oppression around their throats, and they want us to care.

I wonder how many of these people, if placed in the position Cassie Bernall is said to have been in, would have answered yes. If truly put to the test, how many of them would find their faith so comforting, so sustaining, that they would be willing to die for it? Would the same people who routinely use God as a weapon suddenly find themselves unsure? Christians in this country don't know what oppression means. They think oppression is an artist putting a crucifix in a glass of urine, or Terrance McNally writing a play portraying Jesus as gay. They mistake oppression with indignation. Meanwhile, Buddhists in Tibet are slaughtered because they don't fit into the Chinese plan, and our government does nothing to protest. Probably because they're too busy planning their next prayer breakfast.

Six months before the murder of Cassie Bernall, gay college student Matthew Shepard was also killed because of who and what he was. He was dragged from a truck, beaten, and left tied, crucifixion-like, to a fence post in the bitter cold to die, simply because two men didn't like what he stood for. The comparisons to Jesus are theatrical and easy to make. Maybe too easy. After all, Matthew Shepard wasn't trying to save the world. He wasn't trying to make a statement. He didn't claim to stand for anything. Yet he did stand for something, and he did make a statement, as did Cassie Bernall and her death. Unfortunately, I think most of the religious community missed the point entirely. Bernall's death was portrayed as a result of her innocence, while Shepard's was, some preached, a result of his sin.

I sometimes wonder what I would have done had I been a Jew living during the Holocaust. Would I, if possible, have tried to hide my Jewish heritage to escape almost certain death? Had I indeed been an early Christian, would I have betrayed my religion if doing so meant surrendering my life? I don't honestly know. Faith is a strange thing, convenient when it sustains us, difficult when it singles us out.

So, too, is queerness. Matthew Shepard's refusal to

hide his sexuality ended up killing him, as it does many people each year. Shortly after Bernall's death it killed 14-year-old Jeff Whittington of Wellington, New Zealand, who was kicked and beaten to death by two grown men who didn't like his fingernail polish and purple hair. It also killed Brandon Teena, murdered by men who didn't appreciate the fact that one of "their" girls was sleeping with Teena, a girl who passed as a boy. Shepard, Whittington, and Teena couldn't hide who they were, and they paid for it with their lives. They never had the chance to answer "no" to the question put to them.

I have never been faced with the threat of violence or death because of my queerness. But I still resent the fact that there are people who, if given the chance, would do me harm because queerness is a part of me. I can't honestly claim to understand being the target of oppression. Being white, male, and middle-class makes things pretty easy for me, and it is very rare that I ever feel threatened. But I am always aware of how fortunate I am in this respect, and I know that in certain situations things could change in a moment.

My Sunday school teacher, although I suspect she had different motives for doing so, taught me a valuable lesson: You don't really know what you stand for until you're tested. I wish there were a way to teach it to the Christians screaming about oppression today. Part of me thinks it would do them a world of good to be dragged out of their beds in the middle of the night and forced to confront their beliefs in the way that other people are forced to stand up for who and what they are on a daily basis. It's much easier to cry wolf than it is to put yourself on the line. Then we'd see how willing they are to defend the things they say they stand for. But I'm not sure they would even know what those things really are.

It's Not Mean If It's True

My friend So Young (yes, she's heard all the jokes about it, so don't even go there) comes from a very traditional Korean family. When she was growing up her family went to Korea every other year to visit her mother's relatives. This was a major event but not an entirely welcome one. Because once there, her mother's sisters and their children—all daughters—would congregate in one place to catch up on one another's lives and engage in a ritual that So Young calls "Name That Flaw."

Name That Flaw involved all of the aunts and cousins crowding into the kitchen. The aunts sat around the table, and the girls hovered on the periphery, trying to remain as invisible as possible because they knew what was coming. After some preliminary chitchat, the aunts would gaze around the room at the assembled girls and begin.

Whichever aunt had been selected to go first would choose a girl and sit, looking her over, until she was ready to speak. Then she would make her pronouncement: "Anna is thinner than last time," she might say. "That is good. But she has crooked teeth. Boys don't like that."

As her daughter had been the subject of the initial verdict, it would now be Anna's mother's turn to go. "Jin's eyes are a little too Japanese for my liking," she might say, or, "It is a good thing Karen has such a lovely face, because she is not very bright."

Round and round the table the aunts went, each dissecting the perceived faults of her sisters' children. No woman ever commented on her own child, as that was not allowed. Nor did she automatically choose to judge the daughter of someone who had criticized hers. It was not a competition.

When So Young told me about this family tradition, I asked what had been said about her.

"Last year they said my butt was too big and that I didn't know how to cook rice very well," she said. "I got off pretty easily. They told my cousin Trish that she had a man's feet."

The most interesting thing about this ritual is that none of the aunts saw anything wrong with it. When So Young once questioned her mother about why they did it if it made the girls feel bad, her mother shrugged and said, "It's all true, isn't it? How can it be mean if it's true? We are just pointing out things that need to be corrected, if possible. And, if not, it is still good to know about them."

It's not mean if it's true. There's logic in that. Harsh logic but logic nonetheless. And perhaps a kind of logic we should employ more often. Ours is a culture that doesn't really like hearing the truth very much. We prefer to believe that everything is fine the way it is. In fact, we go out of our way to reassure one another that things are great.

When I was editing children's books a number of years ago, one of the most successful series being published for young readers at that time was called *Coping With*. Each book in the series addressed some issue that children might find themselves dealing with, so there were titles like *Coping With An Alcoholic Parent* and *Coping With Diabetes*. Each book assured the reader that things would be OK and that whatever the given situation was, it was manageable. It was all very Marianne Williamson and empowering.

The running joke in my office was that we should do our own series (*Coping With* was published by a rival company) called *Face It*. The *Face It* series would be similar in scope to *Coping With,* but it would tell the truth. And the truth is that being different really sucks sometimes.

So we wanted to do books like *Face It: You're Fat* and *Face It: No One Likes You*. Instead of doing a lot of hand-holding, these books would give kids practical advice for dealing with a situation that in all likelihood was going to cause them misery. Telling a fat kid that people have different kinds of bodies and that's OK is great, but it doesn't really help him deal with taunts of "Moby Dick!" on the playground. Reassuring a child that her parents' divorce has nothing to do with her doesn't prepare her for the horror of being dragged back and forth between their respective houses for holidays. Much more useful would be chapters like "Why Your Big Ass Is Going to Make It Hard for You to Fit Into Airplane Seats" and "Manipulating Mom and Dad Into Giving You Gifts."

We never did get the *Face It* series off the ground. It

was always more of a fun fantasy than a practical possibility. But there could still be some use for it. Only now I think I'd turn it into a series for delusional adults who don't want to admit what's going on around them. It would be a wonderful way to encourage people to actually look at the issues that affect them instead of pretending they aren't there or that the problem is about something other than what it is.

Imagine, for instance, *Face It: Gays in the Military*. Instead of going on and on about how gay people can be just as loyal and brave as everyone else, we could talk about really crucial issues such as, "Yes, We're Going to Look at Your Dick in the Showers, So Deal With It," and "If You Want Me to Blow You After You've Gone Six Weeks With No Sex, You're Going to Have to Put Out Too." These are the things straight people *really* need to know, the issues they *really* worry about, so we should give them answers. Hiding the truth behind arguments over rights and sensitivity training just muddies it all up.

Another favorite of mine would be *Face It: Queers Have More Fun Than You Do*. This book would outline the ways in which gay people have better lives than straight people. I think chapters such as "Only Other Women Know How to Eat Your Pussy Right," "No Kids Means More Vacations," and "You May Have Marriage, But We Have Bette, Liza, and Barbra" would be just the thing. It would force homophobic readers to realize gay people have really cool lives, and it might help them understand that the reason they treat us badly a lot of the time is because they're jealous.

Not that straight people are the only ones who need a dose of reality. Queers could also use a couple of volumes of *Face It*. One of my absolutely favorite magazines of all time was *Diseased Pariah News*. Born out of the AIDS crisis, this irreverent 'zine gave its readers the information they needed about living with HIV. For instance, the "Get Fat, Don't Die," column offered high-calorie recipes for people trying to counteract the weight loss often associated with AIDS. Essays about how contributors contracted the AIDS virus detailed the ways gay men were (and weren't) responding to the crisis. The writing was sarcastic and (to some people) offensive, but it was always on the mark.

That's what we need more of. If we had *Face It: If Relationships Were Easy We'd All Have Them*, for example, we could address the issues gay men looking for love encounter. "If You Meet Him at a Bar, Don't Be Surprised When It Doesn't Work Out" would be my choice for the opening chapter, followed by "There's More to Love Than Picking Out a Great China Pattern," "No One Likes a Whiner," and "When the Boyfriend Within Is an Asshole." Enough of this pie-in-the-sky relationship nonsense. Give men the cold, hard facts about how it actually works and they might have something they can use.

For our lesbian sisters, might I suggest *Face It: You Have Bad Hair*. This volume would get to the heart of dyke life. Beginning with "You Really *Can* Have Too Many Cats," the book would progress through "Lingerie Is Not Made of Flannel" and "Not Everything Is a Patriarchal Plot" before finishing up with "Just Because She's a Dyke and Plays Guitar Doesn't Mean She Can Sing Well."

And how about *Face It: You're Aging*. Many gay people

do not, sadly, grow up with grace or dignity. We aren't encouraged to. But this book could change that. With chapters such as "No One Your Age Should Wear Shorts That Small," "When It's Your Turn to Stop Tanning," and "Transitioning from Circuit Party Queen to Opera Queen," we could launch a revolution—as long as people take the message to heart.

But I doubt that they would. The human, as a rule, is a delusional species. Asking us to really look at ourselves is asking too much. I suspect, for example, that a book like *Face It: The Gay Community Is a Myth* would not be met with enthusiasm. We have too much invested in pretending that because we're all queer we all like each other and have the same agendas. Just ask the organizers of the March on Washington. It's far easier to force people to embrace a version of reality that, while wonderful, simply doesn't reflect the truth. It's easier to pretend things will be better for *all* of us if the ones who want gay marriage get it, or if the ones who think antidiscrimination legislation will end hate crimes get it, or if the ones who want to be Boy Scout leaders get to do it, than it is to face reality.

And maybe those things would all be great. Maybe I want some of them too. But I know they don't solve things for all of us, and I know some queer people who don't want them just as badly as others do want them. Instead, maybe we should look at some of the fundamental problems facing us as a community struggling to stay together. Maybe we should start by asking ourselves why gay men are so reluctant to support (or even acknowledge) lesbian issues, why almost two decades into the AIDS crisis young gay men are seeing a shocking rise in new cases of infection, or why older queer people are almost invisible in our world. Despite our many gains, some of the basic problems haven't gone away, but we don't often talk about that.

Maybe we need So Young's aunts to herd us into the kitchen and pick us apart. If they do, will we listen? Or will we stare at the floor and think about something else, hoping they'll move on to the next girl so we can try to forget about our fat thighs and bad skin?

The Condensed History of Queer Cinema

Gay men have always had a love affair with Hollywood and the silver screen. Movies have given us our favorite lines, our favorite icons, and our favorite fantasies. The magical combination of stardom, drama, and tragedy that surrounds the world of film is irresistible to us. And even though the majority of movies are made with straight audiences in mind, we know we are the ones who truly keep cinema alive. Without gay men, the movie industry would be a barren wasteland. Oscar night is our equivalent of a presidential election, but it's even better because, let's face it, no political candidate ever looked good in a Halston gown and Harry Winston jewels.

While today we have our very own films and our very own film festivals, this has not always been the case. For the most part, we have had to be content with what Hollywood has given us. Not that this has been a bad thing. Indeed, the history of film is overflowing with memorable moments that have left lasting marks on gay culture. Because it would be unseemly to appear ignorant about our cinematic past, I offer here a handy guide to key moments in the gay movie canon in the hope that it will both edify and add to your viewing pleasure.

1935: Despite what other, clearly ignorant people might tell you, queer cinema is born in this landmark year with the release of *Dangerous*, starring Bette Davis. Although it is not her first film, it is her first hit, and earns her the first of her two Oscars, an event surpassing even the birth of the Christ child in importance.

1939: *The Wizard of Oz* debuts. Shortly after, the popularity of piano bars skyrockets as gay men everywhere insist that "Over the Rainbow" was written especially for them. They think the same thing about the dialogue in *The Women*, released later that year. They are right on both counts.

1950: Despite winning Best Picture and Best Director Oscars, *All About Eve* fails to score a Best Actress statue for its star, Bette Davis. That bitch Judy Holliday wins for *Born Yesterday*, but who remembers *her*? This is a dark time for gay men everywhere, and much weeping ensues.

1959: Closeted gay heartthrob Montgomery Clift stars with fabulous gay icon Elizabeth Taylor in the gay-themed melodrama *Suddenly, Last Summer*, penned by perennially suffering queer writer Tennessee Williams. Despite the obvious, many people completely miss the point, thinking Taylor's character is simply distressed over the oppressive humidity in New Orleans.

1962: Real-life rivals Joan Crawford and Bette Davis

team up for the camp classic *What Ever Happened to Baby Jane?*, uttering some of the most famous lines in movie history. Party banter is changed forever as, "But you *are,* Blanche. You *are* in that chair!" becomes the snipe heard round the world.

1967: The film version of Jacqueline Susann's novel *Valley of the Dolls* purports to show audiences the perils of too many drugs, too much sex, and not enough perox- ide. Gay men, knowing *real* superstar Judy Garland was dropped from the film for being too fucked up to per- form, declare Patty Duke's pill-popping superdiva Neely O'Hara an amateur.

1968: Capping an already-full decade, *Funny Girl* showcases the debut of Barbra Streisand and provides gay men with a new obsession that will take on frighten- ing proportions in the coming decades. Taking a cue from La Barbra, men everywhere change the spelling of their names to things like Marc, Jon, and Robrt.

1970: *The Boys in the Band*, rumored to actually be a documentary of writer Mart Crowley's birthday party, depicts a group of gay men in all their dysfunctional glory. Straight audiences wonder if gay men can really be that bitchy. Gay audiences think this is funny.

1975: *Dog Day Afternoon* features Al Pacino as an insane bank robber trying to get money for his stagger- ingly unattractive lover's sex change operation. Fortunately, that same year Quentin Crisp's *The Naked Civil Servant* shows a true queen in action, although some viewers mistakenly believe that Crisp is played by Bette Davis and nominate her for an Oscar.

1980: Apparently not content with making one terrible portrayal of gay life, Al Pacino stars in *Cruising*, which does for gay sex what the Inquisition did for Catholicism. Luckily, the Village People strike back with *Can't Stop the Music*, providing audiences with a *truly* authentic look at queer culture.

1983: Though its importance to gay cinema is not immediately realized, *All the Right Moves* attracts queer audiences with the presence of soon-to-be-superstar Tom Cruise. When it is discovered that Cruise flashes his manhood, however briefly, the film becomes an instant classic. After the video release, gay men across the country suffer repetitive stress injuries to their thumbs from hitting their pause and rewind buttons repeatedly.

1989: Bette Davis dies, and so does classic queer cinema.

1991: Signaling what some believe to be the opening volley in a gay cinematic revolution, openly queer director Gus Van Sant releases *My Own Private Idaho*. Unfortunately, the marriage of star Keanu Reeves to media mogul David Geffen makes him appear unavailable to fans and the movie does poorly at the box office.

1992: Straight audiences are completely shocked when the heroine of the sleeper hit *The Crying Game* turns out to be a man. Gay audiences are shocked that any self-respecting drag queen would have such awful hair and makeup.

1993: Tom Hanks walks away with an Oscar for his portrayal of a gay man in *Philadelphia*. Straight people applaud his performance, but queer men wonder how his character could possibly be gay and barely touch hunky Latin lover Antonio Banderas.

1998: Seemingly every British actor comes out of the closet simultaneously. Unfortunately, they all look alike, and everyone thinks there is only one of them. In America, Kevin Spacey lobbies desperately to land the lead in the new *Batman* film so that nobody will get suspicious.

1999: Hollywood decides that gay characters are fun, based largely on the success of movies like *As Good As It Gets, My Best Friend's Wedding*, and *The Object of My Affection*. But it is primarily straight audiences who think these films and characters are interesting, and while Tinseltown tries to find the next "big gay thing" to capitalize on the trend, queer viewers head for their local video stores and rent *What Ever Happened to Baby Jane?* and *Funny Girl* instead.

Viagra Falls

"Hey, guess what this is," my friend Sarah says while we're walking to the bus.

I look over. Sarah's tongue is sticking straight out of her mouth.

"Your tongue?" I answer tentatively, thinking maybe it's a trick question.

"No," she says, "a lesbian on Viagra."

I groan, not because the joke is bad, but because I'm all Viagra-ed out. It's all anyone talks about now. It's on every television station I turn to. It's in the papers every day. Why, even Bob Dole went public and announced that taking it had spiced up his and Liddy's sex life. She must be so relieved that she can throw out her Al Gore dildos now.

This is the Year of the Rebuilt Male. First Rogaine went over-the-counter, sending millions of men to drugstores across the nation. Then came Olestra, the fat substitute that makes it possible for us to eat 57 bags of Doritos without gaining an ounce. And now we have this Viagra nonsense. It's like the entire medical industry woke up one day and realized that if American women would spend billions on creams to make their thighs disappear, American men would just as happily empty their wallets to stimulate their follicles and jump-start their prostates.

I guess I should be happy I live in a country that has managed to give men back both their hair and their erections in the same year. I mean, we wouldn't want a bunch of balding impotents to suffer while those selfish women with breast cancer are out partying up a storm. And 85-year-olds scampering around with stiffies must be a great consolation to the folks who can't afford health care for their kids. Little Timmy still needs that inhaler, but at least Grandpa can get it on again.

Luckily for the poor, however, Congress is diligently working to pass legislation that would include Viagra in Medicare and other insurance plans. And then there's that nice man who donated a million dollars to buy Viagra for the underprivileged. Thank heavens. At ten bucks a pill, Viagra is one of those wonder drugs whose soothing pleasures might have remained in reach of only those with deep pockets. Now everyone will have equal opportunities for erections without having to pirate their children's college funds. Isn't that what democracy is all about?

I suppose I shouldn't be surprised about the fuss over this silly pill. This is, after all, a country that spent billions of dollars investigating just exactly where Bill Clinton, who clearly does not need Viagra, had been putting his erection. And while we have all kinds of nifty things to keep women as sterile as Clorox-washed laboratory floors, birth control for men is primarily concerned with how thin we can make condoms so the poor boys who are forced to wear them can still have as much pleasure as possible.

The American public is absolutely in love with the penis, and especially with penises that stand firmly at attention. I've heard rumors that certain members of the government are actively campaigning to make the erection the national symbol, replacing the bald eagle. That barren-pated creature may once have accurately represented our nation of overweight, thinning-haired citizens perfectly, but now that we have hair restorers and Viagra, we need something more virile to signify our collective return to randy youth.

In fact, I think a monument is in order. What better way to commemorate the restorative powers of the century's greatest medical achievement? Surely that clever young woman who did such a nice job on the Vietnam memorial could work something up, perhaps a phallic-shaped tower of rare blue-veined Italian marble. Beginning at the bottom and spiraling upward to the turgid tip would be the inscribed names of all the men whose sagging love lives have been saved by Viagra.

Visitors would flock to this important site. Circling it slowly, they would scan the sides for the names of friends and loved ones. "There's uncle Ken!" smiling children would squeal in delight while taking licks at their Viagra-pops bought from nearby vendors. Once every 15 minutes a fountain, cleverly concealed within the monument, would erupt, showering everyone within a 50-foot radius with life-giving water. Drenched, onlookers would clap and cheer at the wonder of it all.

Eventually, of course, the marvels of Viagra will grow to miraculous proportions. An entire religion will spring up. Worshipers will gather in their temples to rejoice in the God-given gift of eternal erections. Communion will consist of receiving the little blue triangle on outstretched tongues. After consumption, the congregation will celebrate the most holy of unions while singing its praises to the pharmaceutical angels who delivered the gift unto the Earth.

OK, so maybe things won't get that bad. But honestly, what does it say about us as a people that we're making such a big deal over this? We can't manage to educate our children enough so that everyone can read. We can't feed all the people who don't get enough to eat every day. But we can invent a pill that saves us from the horrors of performance anxiety. Surely it will only be a month or two before Andrew Lloyd Webber pens *Viagra: The Musical*, starring a rejuvenated Dudley Moore as the hero and Liza Minnelli as his suddenly happy wife.

And what does it say about our notions of sex that we define lovemaking by whether a man can get hard? If someone invented a pill that ensured women had orgasms every time they had sex (let's call it Niagra), you can bet there wouldn't be a parade or legislation to make it available to everyone. In fact, I'm fairly certain Pat Robertson and his Christian Coalition would immediately hold an emergency meeting to discuss how to handle "Satan's aphrodisiac." Horny women are, after all, a threat to God and national security. It's only when cocks across America are able to function properly that we call it a national holiday.

In all fairness, I should point out that the Viagra craze isn't limited to the heterosexual population. Gay men have already discovered 83 different ways it can be utilized to make sex better. In some circles it's even replaced Ecstasy as the fuel of choice for hours of lovemaking. We may be queer, but we're still men, and we love our dicks as much as our straight brothers love theirs. Maybe even more. How long will it be before the makers of the turn-on tablet come out with a specially marketed pink triangle version?

I think what's scariest about the rejuvenating touch of Viagra is that it's actually a side effect. Viagra is a medication originally designed for patients with heart trouble. It didn't do much for their tickers, but it made them frisky as bunnies. Suddenly what could have been a colossal financial failure turned into the find of the century. I'm all for serendipity in the world of scientific discovery, but this is a little disconcerting. If they didn't know what this stuff would do in the first place, how can they possibly know what the long-term effects might be?

Take, for example, Olestra. It was heralded as the miracle fat substitute. No more fatty calories. No cholesterol. Why, even potato chips could become a health food. Except for that whole slippery sphincter thing. It seems that, in a number of folks, eating Olestra turned their bowels into a replica of a ride at Water World. Emergency rooms across the country filled with innocent people who chowed down on a bag of chips and then cramped severely hours later, or discovered in the middle of their commute home that the nachos they'd enjoyed at lunch were about to come bursting out of their behinds with enough force to launch the Mir space station.

What if Viagra turns out to have similar aftereffects? Already they're warning that taking it in combination with other drugs can be deadly. Suppose we discover that mixing it with something like Diet Pepsi causes the user to wear plaid? The beaches of Fire Island would never be the same. Even worse, what if it reacts with Rogaine and results in an overwhelming desire to bring back trends from the 1980s? Is it coincidence that the Culture Club reunion tour was announced only two weeks after the widespread distribution of Viagra in Los Angeles? I think not.

You'd think, in this day and age, that scientists would be able to use their skills for more worthwhile purposes. We can give people hair and take away their fat. Big deal. I'd be more impressed if someone invented a medication that did something really useful, like cause men to suddenly feel an uncontrollable urge to clean the house. Or how about a pill that caused the taker to crave commitment. Personally, I would be first in line for anything that would enable me to read the newspaper without feeling nauseous. I like to be informed, but too often knowing what's going on in the world leaves me dizzy.

But no. What we get are pills that make our hair and our erections grow. I suppose for some people that's enough. But I wouldn't want to know any of them.

Overeducated Consumer

My life has become a consumer wasteland, and I blame this on Mufara Burapti.

Mufara Burapti is seven years old and lives in Indonesia, presumably in one of the bleaker parts where there is no food, no school, and basically nothing useful apart from a small patch of dirt and a bedraggled chicken. At least that's what I can determine from the bio of Mufara that was sent to me by the child sponsorship organization.

Last year I decided it might be a good idea to sponsor a child. After all, I have it pretty good. I'm not rich by any stretch of the imagination, but I don't have to wait in a line every day for a Red Cross volunteer to hand me a plastic pail full of old rice. I don't work 18 hours a day sewing clothes for discount stores, and only once has anyone shot at me for voicing my political beliefs. Besides, what else can you do with 20 bucks a month that actually achieves something meaningful?

So Mufara came into my life. I did a lot of research before I sponsored her, making sure the sponsorship organization was legitimate, delving into the percentage of donations actually given to the communities being served, and, most important, making sure the organization had nothing whatsoever to do with a religious institution. I wanted my money to build a child's life, not teach her to recite Bible verses until someone hands her a scrap of fish like a trained seal.

Once I started sponsoring Mufara, I was very pleased with myself for doing something socially responsible. I enjoyed learning about her favorite school subject (math) and her favorite pastime (playing ball). I especially liked the cheerful little notes she sent from time to time telling me how much fun it was now that the rainy season had returned and they could drink water again. I read her notes while sitting in my air-conditioned house, downing iced tea straight out of the refrigerator (upon which I had placed the picture of Mufara standing beside her chicken), and I felt my karmic debt lessening with every check I wrote.

But being one of those foolish people who can't leave well enough alone, I decided to see what other areas of my consumer-based lifestyle might need attending to. After all, my experience with Mufara had been a good one, so surely I could gain even greater joy by really getting my act together. In particular, I began to look at the products I was using and researching where they came from and who made them.

Within days, I discovered that I was doing just about everything wrong. The food products I dumped in my shopping cart came, I learned, from hideously evil megacorporations that not only used cheap labor, but loaded their products with every harmful chemical known to science. Even when their business practices were borderline acceptable, a little more digging revealed that they had given enormous sums of money to antiabortion groups, antigay groups, or antienvironmental groups. At the very least, they had killed bunnies to test their products.

The end result is that now I can't eat anything. If it doesn't have some kind of suspicious cancer-causing agent or dye it, then it's probably packaged in something that can't be recycled, rendering it unfit for purchase. And even if it says it's made by an outfit with a wholesome name like Mother's Kitchen Naturals, a little scratching beneath the surface will reveal that behind the smiling maternal face on the box lurks the grim visage of Big Ass Fake Food Manufacturers, Inc.

And it's not just food. Once I started looking, I discovered that pretty much everything in my life is just plain bad. My credit card, for example, has the lowest interest rate currently available, which I discovered by exhaustive research. The problem is that it's issued by the Armed Forces Benefits Association. So while I avoid contributing to the debt problem, I'm supporting the military industrial complex. Every time we drop another bomb on someone, my interest rate drops a percentage point.

My mutual funds are even worse. While clearly I need an IRA so as not be a burden on the social security system in my later years, it seems the only way to achieve a healthy financial picture is to plunk my money into a fund heavily weighted toward tobacco, firearms, and drugs whose costs send the copayments on HMOs sky-high. I tried one of those "green" mutual funds where they only invest in socially responsible companies, but when the value sank and they offered us boxes of

Amazon River Basin granola in exchange for our shares, I sold out.

One by one, the accessories of my life have become taboo. I can't use the phone (too many long distance carriers discriminate against minority communities), can't buy music (record companies are notorious about price-fixing and they exploit their artists) or books (unless they're from independent neighborhood stores, and mine never has what I want), can't feed the dog store-bought food (too many animal by-products), can't use anything disposable (landfills are overflowing), and can't buy any normal clothing (to protest worker exploitation).

And the whole gay issue makes things even more complicated. First we couldn't drink Coors beer because the company had antigay leanings. Then we stopped going to Cracker Barrel restaurants because they were mean to us. And most recently there was a lot of confusion about whether we were supposed to fly American Airlines because someone said the company was bowing to pressure from religious groups and pulling their advertising from gay periodicals. Although now I hear that the Coors folks are our friends (even though the family that owns the company is still rabidly right-wing), and GLAAD is supporting American Airlines and the religious groups are mad at them again, so maybe it's safe to get drunk and fly. Frankly, I'm tried of trying to figure it out, so I'm just staying home.

You can see the potential problems ethical consumerism presents. Once you start, it snowballs. I have enough guilt about driving a Volkswagen (the company once made war machines utilized by the Nazis), but at least that was given to me, so I don't feel like the manufacturer actually got any money from me. Still, I have to run it on fossil fuels, and that makes the part of me concerned about the oil monopoly and the overuse of natural resources a little edgy. Every time I fill the tank, I imagine another penguin giving up its tiny soul in an oil tanker spill so I can drive to the grocery store instead of taking the bus.

To make up for it all, I've turned myself into a one-man army dedicated to righting the wrongs of the planet. I recycle. I compost. I don't buy something unless I really need it. I eat organic cookies and drink juice made only from fruit grown by cooperatives. I boycott companies that are destroying the rain forests and contributing to human rights abuses, and I write letters of protest so that everyone knows just what I think about everything. On the days when I think I can't live without eating an Oreo (too much dye and packaged in nonbiodegradable plastic), I work off my frustration by walking 15 miles to the co-op and loading up on chocolate Rice Dream and tofu pups, which I eat while watching *Seven Years in Tibet* on my generator-powered television, all the while thanking the Goddess that at least one penguin can swim free because I didn't cave in to the evil overlord Nabisco.

Sure, it makes me feel good. Sort of. The scary thing is that, more and more, my life is starting to look a lot like little Mufara Burapti's. My friends say I have a haunted look about the eyes. I haven't yet moved into a hut, but yesterday a chicken ran across the front lawn. I'm living with less and less stuff around me, and I wouldn't be at all surprised to find out that instead of helping Mufara I've become one of the faces the sponsorship organization puts in its plaintive mailings sent out to snag new members. I think I'll draw the line at the little plastic bucket, but who can say? I'll have to see if it's recyclable first.

Endangered Species

I don't have any lesbian friends anymore. Well, they're still my friends, but they aren't lesbians. At least not technically. They're all dating men. OK, not all of them, but a shocking number. So many that I barely have enough of the ones that are still dating women left to field a mediocre softball team.

The first time this phenomenon occurred, I didn't worry too much. It was my friend Tracy. She'd just had a nasty breakup with her girlfriend, and she started spending time with this bass player whose band performed at the bar where she liked to shoot pool. The guy actually looked enough like Tracy's ex that it wasn't completely disconcerting, so I wrote it off as some kind of weird rebound thing that would be over in a month or two, a passing interest like the vegetarianism and yoga phases she went through.

But then Anna started doing it too, which was different. Anna's one of those professional lesbians. She was born with keys to a Subaru clutched in one fist and a recipe for organic hummus in the other, and she went right from Dick and Jane to *Our Bodies, Ourselves*. She's had an assortment of lovers, all of them sporting unshaven legs and armpits.

But now she has a Bob. That's what she calls him. "My Bob." She met Bob at the co-op where she shops. Before we knew it, they were hanging out. That's what Anna calls it. "Hanging out." What this means is that three times a week Bob comes over and they have sex. Heterosexual sex. The kind lesbians don't usually have because it involves other people who aren't lesbians.

I like to think that I am supportive of my friends, but I admit that I don't tolerate change very well. After a few weeks of silence, I finally had to ask Anna why she'd suddenly decided to get a Bob after years of, well, not having a Bob.

"You don't know how hard it is dating girls," she said. "They're so much work. Men are simpler."

I've dated men. Not many, but a few. I can assure you they are not particularly easy things to have around. I suggested as much to Anna.

"Try dating girls," she said. "You'll change your mind."

That's the thing, though. I can't just change my mind. I can't just start dating girls. I did that in college, and that was enough. Most queer boys don't, as far as I know, just decide one day that they're going to give up on men and go the other way for a while. Never has one of my gay male friends called and said, "I don't know why, but I really want to go out with this chick from work."

But more and more, my lesbian friends seem to be doing just that. Some of them do it for a week, or a month, or even just once. "Don't tell anyone," my friend Diana said when she finally broke down and told me about a man she had been seeing secretly for a month, "but I love the sex. It's so nice not to worry about the strap-on falling off."

OK, so I told. At least I changed her name. And it doesn't matter, because they're *all* doing it and no one would dare point a finger because she might be the next to go. One by one, my rug-munching sisters are moving from women-only space into mixed-gender territory. It's kind of like what happened when Lilith Fair came along and all those baby dykes who went to see the Indigo Girls discovered there were some boys who liked Amy and Emily just as much as they did and, hey, maybe it was kind of fun to make out in the L7 mosh pit with someone who wasn't majoring in women's studies at Sarah Lawrence. Suddenly that whole Michigan Womyn's Music Festival and all its matriarchal focus seemed a little on the grim side, especially when Jewel started yodeling and everyone got carried away.

Don't get me wrong. I'm all for expressing the whole of one's sexual persona. But I fear that soon I'll start getting wedding invitations in the mail. "Do we know someone named Cheryl Marie?" I'll ask Dave after opening some pastel envelope overflowing with tissue paper.

"She used to be Spud," he'll remind me. "The bartender at Sappho's Fountain."

Only now Spud's parents will be announcing their joy at her forthcoming marriage to Charles Banks III, and we'll be one more dyke short at our next barbecue. I won't go to the wedding. I just can't. I'd be too tempted to perform an intervention, dragging Cheryl Marie off to the bathroom and forcing her to listen to Janis Ian records over and over until she came to her senses.

Besides, if anyone is getting a crystal punch bowl, it's going to be me.

Maybe this whole disappearing lesbian thing is just a severe case of the grass always being greener in someone else's yard. Like I said, a lot of my dyke friends complain that dating women is simply too much work, and they think men would be easier. "Women always want to process," moaned my friend Jess one evening after another of her notoriously short-lived relationships bit the dust, this time because of her and her former partner's inability to climax simultaneously. "Men just get down to business."

On the other hand, I have a lot of straight friends who tell me they wish they were gay men because we seem to be freer sexually and are generally more interesting all around. "You guys really understand that sex is sex and love is love," my straight friend Alex said to me once. "Me, I have a girlfriend who gets pissed off if I look at other women. Plus, she won't give me head. If I were gay, I'd get head all the time."

Clearly neither Jess nor Alex have dated the men I have. Or dated me, for that matter. If they had, they'd be happy with what they've got. But no one listens to me. So far I have lost seven lesbian friends to heterosexuality this year alone. Even Tracy is still seeing the bass player, and it's been six months. That's a record for her, and not a good sign for those of us who wish she would go back to dating someone without a penis.

To correct this deficit, I think the only solution is to start recruiting players from the other team. Now, historically, it has never been all that hard to get supposedly straight men to experiment. Usually all it takes is a beer or two. But we have enough of them on our side now. I think it's time we started working on their female counterparts. Surely there are lots of currently straight women who can be brought over. It just takes some organized effort.

I suggest, therefore, that as a community we begin an all-out campaign to shore up the ranks. We could plant operatives in places frequented by straight women, like cosmetics counters and aerobics classes, and launch a covert campaign promoting the joys of dyke life. A pamphlet tucked into a shopping bag along with that tube of lipstick or bottle of moisturizer might change someone's life for the better. A phone number scribbled on the back of a receipt might open the door to a whole new world. I don't think I even need to describe the possibilities afforded by health club locker rooms.

Or, like the Mormons, we could send freshly scrubbed missionaries onto the streets, buses, and subways of America to spread the gospel of lesbianism to the unconverted. Frankly, I think a lot of currently straight women would jump at the chance to try something new. While sex with straight men certainly has its appeal, I think it's probably more intriguing when it's not your only option. Blowing that humpy UPS driver might be the wet dream of many a gay man, but I bet his wife gets really tired of hearing, "Take that delivery in the rear, baby." Given the opportunity, she could make jaded dykes like Jess and Diana remember what the fuss was all about in the first place.

Whatever we do, we have to do it soon. Time is running out for many lesbians currently poised on the brink of experimenting with heterosexuality. Sadly, it's too late for my friends. But there's still time to save the lesbians in your life. Help them now, before we wake up and find that they've joined the spotted owl and the three-toed skink on the list of creatures who might not make it through this century. Our community needs to preserve its resources if we're to continue marching boldly into the future. It can't be said often enough: A lesbian is a terrible thing to waste.

Ah-Choo!: A Guide to the New Hankie Code

For years gay men searching for sexual fulfillment have been aided by the convenience of the hankie code. For the unfamiliar, this extraordinary cultural invention involves the wearing of different colored handkerchiefs in the back pocket of one's jeans or, in some circles, leather pants. Depending on the color of the handkerchief and its placement on the left or right side, observers can tell at a glance what one's particular fetish is and whether one enjoys being the top or bottom when partaking of this activity. For example, a gentleman sporting a navy blue handkerchief in his left pocket would not be at all unhappy to find a nice fellow with one in his right, as it would mean the two of them could soon be in bed with the righty requesting of the lefty, "Pound me harder, you big stud." You get the idea.

While this code has worked nicely for some, those of us who would like to identify potential partners by means other than what they do in the bedroom (or back room) are left to our own devices. We frequently choose badly because, frankly, there is no "buyer beware" sticker on the package. This is not fair. So in an attempt to right this wrong, I have developed a new hankie code based not on sexual proclivities, but on general personality traits. As with the other hankie code, when worn on the left the color signifies that the wearer meets the assigned description; when worn on the right it signals that the wearer is looking for such a person. Curiously, the code works as well for lesbians as it does for gay men, so there is finally something we can all agree on.

Green Hankie: Eats only organic produce. Will drag you around the co-op for hours searching for locally grown cilantro and pesticide-free lemons. Takes a multitude of vitamins but is still tired most of the time, requiring numerous visits to acupuncturists, herbalists, and crystal healers, none of whom are covered by a health plan. When on a dinner date, will complain loudly that the nonorganic lettuce in the salad will surely result in a sore throat, but will have no problem eating the entire piece of chocolate cheesecake you ordered for yourself. Advantages: Always has homeopathic remedies on hand for sudden colds, interesting collection of New Age books, makes great smoothies. Disadvantages: Will ban meat from the refrigerator, spends most weekends at self-actualization retreats, listens to music by whiny girl singers.

Yellow Hankie: Amateur activist. Has a membership in every gay group you can imagine, from the Human Rights Campaign to the gay swimming club. Has memorized every acronym imaginable, believes in the educative power of the bumper sticker, and leaves articles clipped from the newspaper on your kitchen counter with salient points underlined. Frequently unavailable for dates due to a heavy schedule of petitioning and volunteering for local gay political candidates. Advantages: Gets invited to parties with pseudocelebrities, able to converse on numerous subjects (as long as they're gay), enthusiastic in bed because sex is seen as a political statement. Disadvantages: Makes moviegoing difficult because of constant boycotts of allegedly homophobic films, tends to accuse friends of holding less evolved opinions, thinks Bette Midler is frivolous.

Red Hankie: Processing junkie. Enthusiastically codependent, and will not hesitate to reassure you that your personality defects are completely normal and most likely the fault of your parents. Has an entire library of self-help books and knows the schedule and meeting location for every conceivable 12-step program. Generally has a degree in social work. Dates will involve talking about how you feel about the previous date. Advantages: Always concerned with your welfare, generally doesn't abuse any substance except Prozac, very organized. Disadvantages: The phrase "How do you feel about that?" quickly becomes tiresome, has many depressed friends who need constant attention and call at odd hours, reminds you of your mother.

Blue Hankie: Enjoys foreign films, particularly when playing in an inconveniently located theater with no parking and surrounded by ethnic restaurants of ill repute. Will frequently tell you that anything made in Hollywood is crap and insist on attending only movies featuring arcane or nonexistent plots, actresses with three names, and children carrying balloons. A typical date will consist of sitting through three hours of subtitles and an additional three hours of exposition, during which you are told as many times as possible that you "just don't get it." Advantages: Selecting a date activity is easy, extreme length of most foreign films renders conversation impossible, seldom recognizes sarcasm. Disadvantages: Wears too much black, refuses to attend Oscar night parties, seldom recognizes sarcasm.

Lavender Hankie: Overly fond of Siamese cats. Probably has at least two, who will sport unsuitable matching names like Melissa and k.d. or Joan and Bette, even if male. Will frequently cancel dates because one or the other of them is sneezing, and will not understand when you ask that the cats not be allowed to sleep on your face at night. Dates will involve neurotically prepared dinners followed by looking at high school yearbooks and hearing endless stories about all of the people in them. Advantages: Tends to be very loyal, enjoys giving back rubs, clean. Disadvantages: Likes to call you "Pussums" in bed, high-strung, allows pets to use sex toys as playthings.

Pink Hankie: Bad poet. Has an entire shelf filled with notebooks of badly rhymed sonnets dating back to the sixth grade, and will spend hours reading each and every one of them to you. Easily breaks into tears while listening to Elton John or Jewel albums and says, "Can you believe how deep that is?" Dates center around poetry slams and exhibits of black-and-white photos of body parts with accompanying text from the work of Sylvia Plath. Advantages: Often has interesting friends, does just about anything sexually, will paint a mural on your dining room wall just for fun. Disadvantages: Works at Starbucks or The Gap because part-time work allows more time for "creating," has tentative grip on reality, will break up with you just to have something to write about.

Orange Hankie: Tanning booth aficionado and gym bunny. Insists that every season is swimsuit season, and always looks the part. Spends hours in the gym, and then even more time in front of the mirror. Comes with a startling array of hair and face care products, and considers the Abercrombie & Fitch catalog acceptable bedtime reading. Dates will involve shopping at J. Crew and repeatedly answering the question, "Does this make my ass look big?" Advantages: Takes a good picture, easy to shop for, likes just about anything. Disadvantages: Has many friends named Kyle, obsessive about fat intake, tends to go downhill rapidly after age 26.

Black Hankie: Depression queen. Medicine cabinet is filled with half-used prescriptions for every mood-altering medication known to science. Stays on each drug for a month before announcing, "It just isn't working" and trying another. Partial to career paths almost certain to result in failure, and frequently laments that it's too late to become a model, write a novel, or learn French, so why bother? Dates will consist of recounting everything said at the last therapy session, and the therapist's reactions. Advantages: Loves Janeane Garofalo, makes your life seem comparatively wonderful, has low expectations. Disadvantages: Misery loves company, won't go outside if sunny, will blame you for breakup.

White Hankie: Virgin martyr. Never does anything wrong, but makes sure that you know when you have. Is adept at sighing and looking disappointed, particularly on birthdays and anniversaries. Passive-aggressive, and will answer almost any question about making plans with, "Well, if that's what you want to do," without suggesting an alternative. Favorite phrase is, "I don't want to talk about it," particularly when uttered while sulking over situations of unclear nature and origin. Dates will revolve around discussions of exes and everything they did to ruin the relationship. Advantages: None. Disadvantages: Reminds you of your mother.

Rainbow Hankie: Professionally gay. Will only see gay movies and plays, read gay books, talk to gay people, shop in gay stores, listen to gay music, and eat in gay restaurants. Tends to originally come from a small homophobic town or have majored in gay studies. Dates will consist of looking in the local gay newspaper and going to whatever happens to be going on, as long as it's thoroughly gay. Advantages: Will hold your hand on the street, great fun at Gay Pride, has extensive collection of gay books and music. Disadvantages: Wears Freedom Rings with everything, will only live in San Francisco or New York, always wants to know, "Is it gay?"

Out of Style

I have straight hair. And no, I don't mean that it won't hold a perm, not that I've ever tried. I mean that it's hopelessly heterosexual.

I've tried to have gay hair. I've gone to expensive salons in the trendy part of town and paid 70 bucks to have my hair "styled" by pouty young men with faux French names. But no matter how much they tease, snip, gel, and blow-dry, it always looks the same. After an hour of fussing and trimming, the weary hairdresser inevitably looks at my reflection in the mirror and says, "Well, it's nice and short."

While other gay men walk down the street with freshly buzzed flattops and stylish George Clooney-inspired cuts, I always looks like I just woke up. Plagued by several inconveniently placed cowlicks, my hair invariably resembles that of a baseball player who has worn his lucky hat for an entire season.

I shouldn't be surprised by this. The truth is, I'm just not very good at the whole gay style thing. For example, I do not look fetching in black turtlenecks. They make me feel as if I'm suffocating, and I spend all day picking at the neck, convinced my throat is closing up. Nor do I make designer clothes look good. They may look great on the mannequins and the models in catalogs, but when I put them on they sag in all the wrong places and look like they came from the 25-cent table at a garage sale.

I have friends who are experts at style. They go shopping and return with three articles of clothing and some fun accessories that can be combined to form 22 different ensembles suitable for any occasion. When I go shopping, I wander around in a daze and come back with some jeans, a flannel shirt, and a pair of wool socks, all of which look exactly like the other jeans, flannel shirts, and wool socks already crowding my drawers. When I display my finds to my friends, they shake their heads sadly while I cringe in shame.

From time to time I'll go out on a limb and try something I've been told is all the rage in gay circles. I should know better. When Marky Mark made Calvin Klein boxer briefs a fetish for homos everywhere, I dutifully bought some. I thought they would be daring. They weren't. They were scary. Marky filled them out beautifully, but on me they resembled some weird kind of diaper. As for my other ill-fated clothing investments, I will say only that the money I spent on those leather shorts would have been better used in my retirement account.

This style deficiency first reared its ugly head in childhood when, after a lot of foot stomping on my part, I was allowed to plan my own wardrobe. It was the early 1970s, a decade marked by the excessive use of colors like lime green and orange, and I still managed some spectacular fashion disasters. For one thing, I was enormously fond of plaids. I don't know why, really, except they seemed cheery. This wouldn't have been so bad if I hadn't also liked stripes.

Many were the mornings when I would arrive at the breakfast table clad in some shocking combination pulled from the drawers of my imagination. My father, equally inept, inevitably told me that I looked "sharp." My sisters, a decade older and experts at creating winning ensembles, would beseech me to go find something less blinding. But I refused, and off to school I'd go, looking like some kind of demented golf pro in miniature. I was never sent home, which I can only attribute to the teachers wanting to see what I would come up with if left unchecked.

As I got older, I began to realize that my fashion knowledge, or lack thereof, was a problem. My peers arrived on the first day of school dressed in the latest trends, and I did not. If they were wearing Levi's, I had on Wranglers. If they marched down the halls in sparkling white Reebok tennis shoes, I was in red Keds. A pretty picture, I was not.

For a long time I thought I'd grow out of it. All the other gay boys seemed at some point to lose their awkwardness and become the fashion plates everyone expected them to be. I still remember the day during my freshman year in college when my friend Jim and I were walking through the mall and he came to a dead stop in front of a store. "Oh, my god," he said, staring at a pair of black shoes with chunky soles and buckles on the side. "Those would look so cute with that shirt I saw in the window at The Gap. Oh, and those pants from J. Crew. Hold on." Half an hour later, he walked out of the mall looking like an ad for Homo America. It was his turning point.

I, on the other hand, stumbled through college in a jumble of baggy pants and ill-fitting sweaters. Finally, I just gave up and adopted the flannel shirt–and-jeans look that I continue to wear to this day.

While I've come to terms with my dressing disability and am generally happy with my basic wardrobe, it doesn't go over well with everyone. When we were shooting the cover of my last book, my editor had the brilliant idea to put me on it. Just me. And a big picture too. The whole front cover. Not just one of the little ones they usually stick on the back. I put up a huge fight, but in the end I lost.

The photographer doing the shoot called me the night before and left a message saying, "Bring a couple of different things to wear." To me, this translated to, "Bring all five of the blue shirts hanging in your closet."

But I started to worry that they wouldn't be good enough. To counter this fear, I actually went to a store and bought some new shirts. I thought they looked fine, and was pleased with myself for having done something fashion forward. When I arrived at the photographer's studio the next day, I laid out my wardrobe and waited for him to be impressed and possibly unable to choose just one from all of the stunning possibilities.

Instead, he looked them over for a moment, and then unbuttoned his own shirt. "Here," he said, handing it to me. "Put this on." Humiliated, I did, and for the next two hours he stood shirtless while taking photos of me wearing his clothes.

I could probably live with my badly dressed self if people would stop reminding me about it. But now there are catalogs especially for gay men, and I feel even worse. I should throw these things away when they appear in my mailbox, but of course I don't. Instead, I sit turning the pages and looking at the men wearing interesting clothing as if it were the easiest thing in the world to do. On them, nipple-revealing tank tops look natural. On me, they look like halter tops. And the models sport multi-colored Freedom Rings with aplomb, making both a fashion and a political statement. On me they hang like some decrepit rainbow. The catalog people lean jauntily against their kitchen counters, cheerfully eating cereal while wearing only silk pajama bottoms. If I did that, I'd have milk stains on my crotch within seconds.

Still, I can't help looking at people I will never be wearing clothes I will never wear. I stare at them sitting in bed with their equally fashionable lovers, pulling playfully on one another's socks. I stare at them running around outside with their golden retriever, whose fur is as shiny and bouncy as that of his masters. And then I look down at my tattered old boxer shorts and over at my dog with his grimy fur and wonder where we went wrong.

Fashion disaster that I am, it's probably a good thing that I can stay at home and write for a living. If I had to go out into the world, I wouldn't know what to wear. I don't own a suit, or even a dinner jacket. I can't remember how to tie a tie, since I haven't had to wear one since Easter Sunday the year I was eight. There is nothing in my closet even remotely resembling "dressy" shoes.

After dressing like a frat boy for so long, I live in fear of being invited to anything that requires clothing that does not come in just small, medium, or large. In fact, I have this recurring dream where I've been nominated for an Oscar for some breathtaking screenplay I've written. Everyone loves it, and there's no doubt I'll win. It's the moment I've dreamed of for years. Only I can't go because I don't have anything to wear. None of the current hip designers want me to sport their latest creation because they know I'll make a mess of it. Left with the contents of my closet, I'm forced to ascend the stage in scuffed-up work boots, jeans, and a faded L.L. Bean shirt I threw on before rushing out the door.

"He can't be gay," the spectators whisper to one another as the horrified award presenters, dripping with style, try to hustle me quickly offstage. "Look at that hair."

What a Concept

Recently, while visiting Los Angeles, I was taken to several art galleries by my friend Mike, who knows a great deal about such things. I am not generally up for encountering art, preferring the gift shops of museums to actually perusing the alleged treasures hung on the walls. But Mike assured me it would be fun and that nothing would be expected of me. And that lunch awaited me afterward. Encouraged by the thought of food, I dutifully went along.

We went to a number of galleries, each filled with art more dramatic than the last. We saw sculptures and paintings and photographs, and were assured by the thin, busy people who hovered around us at each place that the artists whose work we were looking at were very, very happening. I'm sure they must have been telling the truth, because the price tags would have been cruel jokes otherwise, and if there is one thing of which I am certain, it is that contemporary art may be many things, but it is seldom ironic.

Not wanting to appear ignorant in front of so many tanned people wearing sunglasses indoors, I politely nodded and smiled. But when Mike and I entered a cavernous room hung floor-to-ceiling with hundreds of squares of transparent film upon which tiny black-and-white squiggles had been painted, I had to speak up. Especially when I glanced at the price sheet sitting on the gallery manager's desk and saw the little squares of film were selling for $1,100 a pop.

"A thousand bucks for a little piece of clear plastic with some squiggles on it?" I asked Mike, who nodded. "And some of them don't even have squiggles on them," I protested. "They're blank. All she did was take them out of the package and hang them up next to the others. Why would anyone pay $1,100 for something you could pick up yourself at an art supply store?"

"It's not about the little squares of film," Mike explained patiently. "It's about the concept they represent."

"They're blank," I said stubbornly.

"Yes," said Mike. "Negative space. They're a part of something larger, and the blank ones are just as important as the ones with squiggles on them. More important maybe. This artist is very hot right now."

I tried to get into the spirit. I imagined buying one of the blank pieces of film and taking it home. "See that," I would tell people at my next party as they stood around admiring my little square of nothing. "That is a very important artistic concept."

But because I don't have $1,100 to spend on anything, let alone art, I will never know how it might feel to own one of those little empty film squares. I did, however, find myself wondering if the same logic that apparently applies to art in Los Angeles could be applied to certain areas of my life. I decided to give it a shot. A week later my agent called. "Why did you send me 300 sheets of blank paper?" she asked suspiciously. "You were supposed to send me your new book."

"I sent you something even better," I explained patiently. "I sent you the concept of my new book. See, the reader can look at those pages and imagine anything he wants to. That way he'll be intimately involved in the artistic process. It will be a cocreation."

"I can't sell 300 sheets of blank paper to a publisher," she said. "I need something with words on it."

"You're supposed to envision the words," I said, as if talking to a small child. "It's all about the concept of writing. The actual writing isn't important. Concepts are very hot right now."

"Fine," she said. "When you get paid with a concept of a check, don't come whining to me."

Undaunted by her lack of enthusiasm, I launched into my new conceptual life. I imagined that I was a hugely successful writer of concepts, selling my ideas for novels, films, and television shows for millions of dollars. I woke up each morning brimming with new concepts. I became so good at it, in fact, that I was able to conceive an entire day without ever leaving the bed. I did hours of conceptual work while I watched television and ate bowl after bowl of Lucky Charms. At night I threw lavish conceptual parties where my new conceptual friends told me how brilliant I was.

My greatest achievement, however, came when I created the concept of a new boyfriend. I figured that the real thing was too much effort. But with a conceptual lover, I could have exactly what I wanted. I conceived him at 6' 2" and 220 pounds, with dark hair and eyes. I met him, conceptually, at one of the parties I threw for my latest novel concept, which he thought was witty beyond words. It was love at first sight, and we became inseparable.

"It's been so nice," I told my friend Katherine after my conceptual boyfriend and I had been going out for a few days. "We never fight, and he always knows just what I want."

"How's the sex?" she asked.

"Amazing," I said. "I just rub lube all over the sheets and enjoy the concept of intimacy."

My conceptual relationship flowered. Without having to worry about actually calling someone before going to bed, remembering his birthday, or trying to organize our schedules for weekend activities, I got a lot of conceptual writing done. My conceptual boyfriend didn't mind at all that the dog slept on the bed, or that I didn't always want to do what he wanted to do. It was heaven.

Until the money ran out. My agent was right—no one wanted to pay for my conceptual manuscript. And the electric, gas, and phone companies cruelly informed me that while the concept of utilities was indeed free, the real thing was going to cost me. I thought about asking my conceptual boyfriend to loan me some cash, but suddenly I saw him for what he was—a good idea that, upon closer examination, proved to be mere whimsy. He might have been all the rage in certain parts of Los Angeles, but in the real world he was just a vague and not very useful idea.

I wonder if someone would pay $1,100 for him.

Green-Eyed Monster

Well, I have finally succeeded in finding something about Dave that I don't like: He doesn't get jealous. Never. Or if he does, he never lets on, which is even more infuriating than not getting jealous in the first place because it means he's doing it on purpose.

I can't stand this. For one thing, I don't think it's natural. For another, it's totally beyond my own emotional capabilities, a fact I resent deeply. I don't think being with someone more mentally healthy than I am is good for me. Then again, as my friend Amanda helpfully pointed out to me this morning, Sybil was more mentally healthy than I am. I think she only said it because she's gained some weight, but I am kind enough not to mention such things. At least not to her face.

I noticed this trait of Dave's when living in different cities forced us to spend most of our time on the phone. He would mention something totally innocent, like he was going out with friends later, and I would feel stirrings of resentment that I couldn't be there with him. But whenever I would mention going out with *my* friends, he'd say, "That sounds fun. Have a good time."

At first I thought he was playing it cool, trying to

impress me with his nonchalance. I hoped that when we hung up he would storm around a little and think horrible thoughts about my friends, wondering if I liked them better than him. But if he did, I could never tell from his voice.

Then he did the unthinkable. He refused to be annoyed about my sexual past. I am one of those horrible boyfriends who likes to believe that, before meeting me, my lover had a sex life that was barren and unfulfilling. I don't like to think of him as ever having been as excited to see someone else as he is to see me, or feeling lust for anyone but me. I don't care that he didn't even know I existed at the time of his transgressions. He should have held out, even if I didn't.

At the same time, I want to know everything about his exes. I want to know what he has and hasn't done so I can come up with something new that will be a first of some kind. What I really want to know, of course, is how good they all were in bed and whether I have a bigger penis, but I can hardly say that without seeming clutchy. So instead I pry details out one at a time until I have the whole picture. This is an agonizing procedure, but I get from it the same satisfaction I once got from forcing my only somewhat loose teeth to come out when I was a child.

One of the first times we got together, Dave and I were talking (I have no idea why) about what we carried in our wallets. He pulled his out and showed me the contents. Among the assorted credit cards and ATM receipts was a picture of his ex-boyfriend. He showed it to me briefly and moved on as though it were no big deal.

I am one of those men who, when I end a relationship, immediately gets rid of anything that even remotely reminds me of the ex. Pictures. Letters. Underwear. Ticket stubs from first dates. Everything. I have been known to avoid pasta for months after breaking up with an Italian. I don't care to be reminded of men I no longer want to find naked in my bed.

I tried not to be annoyed at Dave about the picture, but I was, even though I knew he had absolutely no interest in his ex. I wanted him to be as thorough about ending things and cleaning house as I am. Had it been me, I would have had that picture in the trash moments after the breakup. I harbored dark suspicions that maybe things weren't as over as he'd told me they were. I also wondered if he'd notice if I took the picture out and threw it away while he was sleeping. To my credit, I did not. Instead I brooded.

Dave never broods. He is so not jealous that he doesn't even worry about me when we're apart. See, I'm fine when we're together or when we're on the phone, because then I know exactly what he's doing. He, on the other hand, doesn't care what I'm doing.

"If you call and I don't answer, don't you wonder where I am?" I asked him one night.

"Not really," he said. "I just figure you're out."

"But don't you ever wonder *who* I might be out with or *what* I might be doing?" I pressed, determined to get something out of him.

"No," he said. "You always tell me anyway."

His calm was beginning to irritate me. "OK," I said tensely. "But don't you ever wonder if maybe, on one of these occasions when I'm out with other people, I might be *doing* something with them? You know, something I usually only do with *you*?"

"Oh, no," he said, as if I'd just asked the stupidest question in the world.

"Why not?" I demanded.

"Because I trust you," he said simply.

This, of course, was totally unfair. You don't tell a man that you trust him. That's insane. No one trusts men. I don't. I know how they are. I know how I am. Or how I could be if I put my mind to it.

Actually, I do trust Dave. I really do. But it's much more satisfying and fun to think about what he *could* be doing and how I *might* react when I found out about it. One night when I knew he was out at his local bar with his friends, I imagined him hooking up with a man who had been after him for months. I pictured them in various sexual acts, and then imagined Dave calling, in tears, to tell me about it so I could have the satisfaction of saying, "I knew all along you would do this."

When he *did* call me later that night, I said, "Well, I hope you're proud of yourself." I'd forgotten that he hadn't really called me earlier and confessed.

"You've been worrying again, haven't you?" he said, and sighed.

See, he even understands my neuroses. Not only that, but he thinks it's sweet. If I didn't know better, I'd accuse him of trying to make me jealous just because he likes it. Heaven knows I've done that. But he never takes the bait. If I tell him that some man at the gym cruised me, he just wants to know what the guy looked like. If I tell him about some particularly choice moment in my sexual past, he only wants to know if we can try the same thing sometime. He's impossible.

A therapist friend suggested that the reason Dave's

trusting nature bothers me is because I'm afraid of what *I* might do when it comes to cheating. But I don't think that's it. I'm not the cheating kind. I think my friend Chloe's analysis is closer to the truth: "He's a man," she said. "And we all know that men are supposed to suck. Ask any straight woman. Only he doesn't suck, and you're having a hard time believing it."

Chloe knows what she's talking about. She's been married for a dozen years to a man who doesn't suck. In fact, her husband doesn't even think about other women while they're having sex. She knows because she asked him, and he's incapable of lying.

"I think about other men during sex all the time," she told me. "But he says I'm all he needs. Can you imagine anything more disturbing?"

She's right. It is disturbing. And she's also right that Dave doesn't suck. I'm very happy about that. But I can't help wanting him to be just the tiniest bit sucky sometimes. Maybe on my birthday or something. Just one day a year I want him to throw a little tantrum because someone flirted with me, or get huffy because he's afraid that if I go out drinking with my friends, after two or three beers some long-smoldering flame will suddenly spark up and I'll do something that requires tears and apologies when I get home.

I don't think he will, though. If he was going to do that, he would have done it at already, before we became so sure of each other (or at least before he became so sure of me). Instead I let myself get good and worked up about some imagined indiscretions and then I think about what it would be like to tell him good-bye and throw out everything that reminds me of him.

And then I imagine myself on a date afterward, showing some other man what's in my wallet. When I open it, a picture of Dave falls out, and immediately I know I've made the biggest mistake of my life. For a moment I'm horrified at how stupid I was. Then I remind myself that it's all a daydream. I pick up the phone and call him to tell him that I love him. If he knows what's good for him, he'll be there to answer it.

Thou Shalt Not Have Any Common Sense

A while back, largely as a result of the shootings at Columbine High School and other schools across America, the House of Representatives passed an amendment making it legal for publicly funded schools to post that classic document of Christian morality, the Ten Commandments, within their halls and classrooms. Never mind that this goes completely against the whole separation-of-church-and-state principle. The wise old white men who run our country think that if kids see the commandments every day, it will stop the increase in youth violence. Not that they have any actual proof to back this up. It's just a theory. As a friend of mine was told by his representative when he called to ask how the man could possibly vote for such a thing, "It can't hurt."

I'm not so sure about that. Have you read the Ten Commandments? Apparently the members of the House haven't. Because if you look at the holy ten, they have very little to do with kids—or anyone else—killing each other. And the fact that they're being set forth by politicians as a model of ethical behavior is stunning. Observe:

The First Commandment:
Thou shalt have no other gods before me.

OK, fine, the Ten Commandments were originally a covenant between the Israelites and their God, kind of a prenuptial agreement outlining what a person had to do to be one of the Chosen Ones. Of course, God didn't want anyone else honing in on the action; that's only fair. But what about all those Hindus and pagans and Buddhists? Do they have to nervously pretend to go along with the whole one God concept or face being blamed for everything that goes wrong? It wouldn't be the first time. But since most of the House is made up of Christians of one kind or another, it might not have occurred to them that this could inconvenience anyone.

The Second Commandment:
Thou shalt not make unto thee any graven
images.

Well, I don't think anyone has suggested melting down the contents of the U.S. Mint to make a golden calf or anything, so this probably isn't a big worry. But I suppose some kid will sacrifice a goat beneath a Marilyn Manson poster one of these days and then we'll never hear the end of it. Or maybe instead of building a whimsical little float out of chicken wire and tissue paper for homecoming, a couple of cheerleaders who traded their souls to the dark side in exchange for spots on the varsity squad will craft a statue of Satan and go on a killing spree to repay their evil debt. People have done less to get a pair of pom-poms.

The Third Commandment:
Thou shalt not take the name of the Lord thy God in vain.

Damn it. This takes all the fun out of everything. But we still have *shit* and *fuck* to get us through. I wonder, though, if swearing is truly a problem. I don't see the connection between letting out a few *goddamns* and suddenly wanting to off the entire football team because they called you a faggot one too many times. I think maybe we need more swearing, not less, especially in government. I, for one, would love to see the president turn to the Chinese leaders during a summit meeting and say, "We're not giving you a fucking thing until you ignorant little peckerheads get your goddamn asses out of Tibet. Got that?" And I can guarantee more folks would watch political discussions if they could hear someone say to Bay Buchanan, "Maybe if you got laid more, you homely bitch, you wouldn't be so uptight."

The Fourth Commandment:
Remember the Sabbath day and keep it holy.

No work on the weekend. Big deal. It just gives all those kids planning to blow up their schools more time to build bombs in their garages. Sure, you could drag them off to church for the day, but that's just going to make them even more determined. Nothing will send a disturbed kid over the edge faster than having to sing "Kumbayah" while holding hands with a lot of other pimply faced teenagers trying to channel their sexual frustration into religion. Trust me. I've been there. Besides, kids are barely in school enough as it is. If you really want to keep an eye on them, do away with summer vacation.

The Fifth Commandment:
Honor thy father and thy mother.

Finally, five commandments into it and we have an almost sensible one. Not giving your parents cause for worry is a worthy aspiration, if only because you want them to leave you alone. But since every single parent of a kid who's gone on a shooting spree has looked into the television camera afterward and said, "He was such a good boy and never gave us any trouble," I have my doubts about familial respect tempering antisocial behavior. And again, I think it's just a tad ironic for politicians to be encouraging children to emulate their elders. Look what it did for the Kennedys.

The Sixth Commandment:
Thou shalt not kill.

This, of course, is the big one, and who could argue with it? Not killing other people is pretty much a given. But do you really have to *tell* people this? Isn't it something you just know, the same way you know that poking yourself in the eye with a sharp stick will hurt, or that wearing white after Labor Day is a no-no and that you should expect to be severely mocked if you choose to do so? Unless the wiring in your brain is on the fritz, you're probably going to recognize that causing other people to stop living is a Bad Thing. And if something has made you so fucked up that you don't realize that, seeing it written on a sign in homeroom isn't likely to change your mind. Besides, I can't help finding it curious that the government of the last country in the Western world that still allows capital punishment really thinks hearing "Thou shalt not kill" repeatedly is going to make a difference. Maybe they could amend it to say "thou shalt not kill unless the person comes from a minority group or can't afford good lawyers." Then at least they wouldn't appear quite as hypocritical.

The Seventh Commandment:
Thou shalt not commit adultery.

Well, let's see. The man who was president when all of this hoo-ha started didn't seem to have a problem with this one, so why should the rest of us? If a little nooky on the side is good enough for the leader of the free world, it's good enough for the unwashed masses. Having the government throw this one in our faces reminds me of the infamous Michael Bowers, the former attorney general of Georgia who fought tooth and nail to uphold that state's antigay sodomy law while simultaneously carrying on a ten-year adulterous affair. And honestly, if these angry kids were getting laid more often, they probably wouldn't be so angry and feel the need to off one another. I can't prove it, but I bet every single kid who has ever gone on a killing spree was a virgin when he did it.

The Eighth Commandment:
Thou shalt not steal.

Another one that seems perfectly logical, but I don't really know what this has to do with school violence. I guess what they mean is that kids shouldn't steal the guns they use to kill each other. Good thing there are pawn shops and Wal-Marts that sell them cheap. Or they can just borrow them from their parents. And since when is the government worried about stealing? If they're so concerned about it, I have three words for them: *campaign finance reform*.

The Ninth Commandment:
Thou shalt not lie.

Wow, government and religious leaders lecturing us about lying. Just look at the fine role models they've given us over the years. A friend of mine once said, as we were standing in line on election day, "I always vote for the one who tells the best lies." Lies are what our country is founded on. If you don't believe me, ask a Native American. And anyway, I don't think not lying will stop kids from going postal. In fact, as far as I know, none of the kids involved in these shooting sprees has lied about it. If anything, they've left very detailed plans and explanations of their motives.

The Tenth Commandment:
Thou shalt not covet.

I'm told by a priest friend that this means we should all be happy with the lives that we have and not be envious of what our neighbors have because it leads to ill will. But since the vast majority of teen shooters have been middle-class white boys from the suburbs, I'm not sure what it is they're supposed to be coveting. Poverty and discrimination? These kids aren't shooting each other over sneakers or girlfriends; they're shooting each other because they're frustrated and angry. But it's easier to blame it on sneakers and girlfriends.

In the end, I'm afraid the infamous ten don't provide much in the way of useful instruction, at least when it comes to stopping violence among young people. Not that it matters. If the politicians who think religion is going to save us looked back in time, they'd find that the greatest horrors in human history were perpetuated by people who claimed to be living out religious principles. Slavery. The Crusades. White supremacy. Homophobia. They were (and still are in some cases) all justified using religion, even if the justifications are based on a twisted interpretation of religion that has to be blamed more on the people preaching than on the teachings themselves.

I do think it's a good idea to teach kids solid morals. But we're looking in the wrong place. I think there should be just one commandment: Leave Everyone Else Alone. But I'm just one guy, not a whole religion, so I'll probably have to direct our lawmakers elsewhere. Ironically, given the current hysteria being waged by certain members of the House against pagan groups practicing on military bases, our leaders might do better to take a look at the Wiccan Rede, the fundamental tenet of witchcraft. "An it harm none, do as you will," says the Rede. Sounds good to me. Can you see it on posters in America's schools? It couldn't hurt.

Et Tu, Po?

Poor Tinky Winky. He's been dragged out of the closet. As his handlers try and do damage control to save his career, the world watches and wonders whether children's television will ever be the same.

Personally, I wasn't shocked by the revelations of Tinky's sexual leanings. By now the Tubbies and their peculiarities are well known to almost everyone. But I had my suspicions from the very beginning. Back when the Teletubbies first invaded American shores from Britain, I heard a lot about them, primarily from my friends who have toddlers and spend a lot of time watching television in the mornings. After hearing unanimously positive reviews, I decided to check them out.

The first show I saw began with a disembodied Voice intoning, "One day in Teletubby land, it was Po's turn to wear the skirt." Finding this intriguing, I watched to see what would happen.

A moment later, Po wandered on-screen and encountered the skirt, which appeared mysteriously in a patch of flowers. In reality, it was actually a tutu. A pink tutu of the kind worn by little girls who take ballet and listen to *The Nutcracker* with alarming frequency.

Po was happy to have the skirt. So happy that she did a little dance. Then the Voice announced that it was Tinky Winky's turn to wear the skirt. The Voice frequently booms out of nowhere to tell the Tubbies something exciting is happening. It's a little bit creepy, like God talking to the Israelites or something. But the Tubbies don't seem to care, and they do whatever the Voice tells them.

So Po relinquished the skirt to Tinky Winky, and Tinky Winky did another dance, more in the Martha Graham style than Po's carefree twirling. Then the Voice declared that it was time for Laa-Laa to assume the garment. Laa-Laa, I have since learned, thinks everything is more wonderful than words, and this held true for the skirt. Laa-Laa's skirt dance was indeed wondrous, and it was almost sad when the Voice said it was Dipsy's turn.

Dipsy, however, was not happy about getting the skirt, and ran from Laa-Laa when presented with it. He had to be chased into the Teletubby house before he would put on the skirt. Once he did, however, he did quite an amazing number before removing it and leaving it on the grass while he ran off to do something else.

I don't think I need to point out to queer readers why I found the whole skirt incident so interesting. Frankly, this is *not* the sort of thing one generally sees on a show for young people, even a show that airs on PBS. I was thrilled, and began watching regularly. For the next week, I tuned in as the Teletubbies engaged in all kinds of curious activities, from sailing across a magical pond in boats to washing themselves with giant sponges. With each new episode, my suspicions grew.

Things got even better when I found out about Tinky

Winky's purse. See, I decided to visit the official Teletubby web site, where I discovered that each Tubby had her or his own biography. According to Tinky Winky's write-up, his favorite belonging "is his bag, which he likes to take out with him for walks." Now, I know that in Britain they sometimes use different words than we do here in America. Our elevator, for example, is their lift. I can only assume that *bag* is another example, because what Tinky Winky has is definitely a purse. Maybe a handbag. But it is certainly not a bag of the sort one gets for, say, purchasing groceries or becoming a member of one's local public television station.

This was all too much. I know the Tubbies, as characters, are supposed to behave like the two-year-olds who are their audience. They frequently hug and shriek and act like mad queens, but so do most kids that age. But I find it hard to believe that all of these things add up to mere coincidence. Let's face it: When the Tubbies line up and wave, they look like a living rainbow flag rippling gaily in the wind. I knew after a few shows that I was witnessing the arrival of the first gay role model on children's television. Then I waited for the inevitable backlash.

I didn't have to wait long. Tinky Winky was outed shortly thereafter. The show's creators, of course, have denied that the Tubbies have any sexuality whatsoever, but parents are still rushing their distraught offspring to therapy. In all the excitement surrounding the "Is he or isn't he?" debate, however, something has been overlooked: Who leaked the story to the press? Those of us in the know were keeping it to ourselves, afraid that if word got out there would be hell to pay. At first we all blamed Jerry Falwell, but now he says he didn't do it. And if not good old Jerry, then who?

I'm tempted to blame Bill Clinton. After all, what could better overshadow his Oval Office activities than a scandal involving a beloved icon of toddlers everywhere? But I don't think even Slick Willie is that big of a scumbag.

I think the source is much closer to home. In all the furor, no one has really asked the most important question: What might the other Tubbies have to do with this?

The case against Tinky Winky is, even I admit, purely circumstantial. He's lavender. He has a gay-pride–like triangle antenna. He carries a purse. OK, so that's pretty damning evidence. But he's never said a word about his preference, and there's no photographic evidence. So while we're taking a good, hard look at what Tinky Winky's hidden message might be, why not also look over his three cohorts to see what might be lurking beneath their smiling, big-eyed exteriors?

Dipsy is the next-biggest Teletubby, and second in line for control of the merry band. A weird fluorescent green color, he sports an antenna of undeniably phallic design. Pointing straight and tall, it wobbles grotesquely about his head as he races through Teletubby Land. It doesn't take a rocket scientist to see that he's some kind of pagan phallic god, a throwback to the pre-Christian days when people wantonly worshiped the forces of nature and danced around maypoles in the expectation that doing so would bring bountiful crops and pregnant farm animals. Has Dipsy come along to undermine centuries of church indoctrination? Is he exacting revenge for the forced skirt-wearing fiasco? I wouldn't put it past him.

Then we have Laa-Laa. Lemon yellow, she delights

in singing a strange song reminiscent of Grace Slick's warbling in the 1960s classic "White Rabbit." Her eyes are frequently half-closed as she traipses among the bright talking flowers of Teletubby Land while playing with her favorite toy, a ball that mysteriously grows larger and smaller at will. Laa-Laa watches her ball and giggles while her antenna, a bizarre pointer that loops around on itself, mesmerizes viewers. I have only one thing to say about this Teletubby: Acid Queen. She doesn't want you to say no—she wants you to tune in, turn on, and drop out.

And finally there's cute little Po. The youngest Tubby is bright red. Her antenna is O-shaped. Her favorite activity is zooming around on a scooter, babbling "faster, faster, faster" and "slower, slower, slower." If you ask me, this little Tubby is the Scarlet Whore of Babylon. If that antenna of hers isn't an open invitation to lust, I don't know what is. And her veiled scooter commands are obviously repressed sexual desires.

With their hidden agendas clearly at stake, any of the three remaining Teletubbies could have reason for throwing Tinky Winky to the wolves. Perhaps Po, sick of being the fag hag of Teletubby Land, decided to give herself more air time. Maybe Dipsy, with his emphasis on macho maleness, couldn't hide his homophobia any longer and wrote an anonymous note after Tinky Winky refused to service him on demand. Then again, maybe Laa-Laa took one too many magic mushrooms from the Forest of Make-Believe and simply talked to the wrong people.

They all have their motives for wanting Tinky Winky out of the way. And so do many other children's television stars. I wouldn't be surprised to find out a Muppet is behind it all. Perhaps, much as Tonya Harding hired thugs to take out Nancy Kerrigan, Big Bird or Grover slipped a few bucks to someone to knock the Tubbies down a few points in the Nielsens. Or maybe the sexually ambivalent Blue of the increasingly popular *Blue's Clues* feared someone would comment on her unusual living situation with Ms. Telephone and decided to shine the spotlight elsewhere.

I think Tinky Winky is the victim of backstabbing. Not since Pee Wee Herman was found pleasuring himself in an adult theater have the mighty come under such intense scrutiny. And where are Tinky Winky's supporters? Bert and Ernie continue their "no comment" strategy. Kermit has extended his vacation in Key West to avoid reporters' questions. And not a word has been uttered by the other Teletubbies.

Sure, the people of West Hollywood have issued a proclamation in support of Tinky and his sexuality. There's even talk of making him the grand marshal of this year's Pride parade. And Miss Piggy said she'd still be willing to do love scenes with him no matter what his personal leanings. But what price will Tinky Winky ultimately pay? Will he find himself only able to get bit parts as the "funny uncle" in *Scooby-Doo* remakes? Or will he, like Ellen and Anne, flee Hollywood in frustration. I shudder to think.

Let's hope that a promising career won't be cut short by this obvious case of mudslinging. With any luck, like *Dr. Quinn's* outed Chad Allen, Tinky Winky will be allowed to continue doing the fine work he has done so far in his short career. I only hope that whoever outed him is able to live with him or herself. Po, are you listening? Because you and your big round O might be the next to fall.

It's All in the Cards

I can't believe it's that season again. No, not tax time. Even worse. I'm talking about that dreaded annual chore: holiday cards. Every year, on November 1, I wake up with a tight feeling in my chest, knowing that the time has come again.

It used to be easy. I only had a couple of friends. Each year all I had to do was buy a single box of cards and send them out. It was kind of fun, actually. I'd wait until some holiday-themed television show was on and then sit there for an hour or so, writing out cards and thinking about how nice it was to know people.

But as I've gotten older, I've accumulated a lot more friends and acquaintances. I now have several lists of people who expect to receive cards. Every year I try to pare the lists down. I go over them, weeding out the editor who didn't buy anything from me or the former friend who said my last book wasn't all it could have been. Generally I can cut a good two dozen or so from the list, and for a minute or two I feel as if I might have a handle on it all.

Except then I have to add the new people, starting with all the men I think might ask me out if I bribe them with a holiday greeting. Then there are the editors who I desperately want to buy things from me, the photographer who took the only good picture of me in existence, and the dog's latest vet. It goes on and on, and when I'm finished, there are always more new names than deleted ones.

As maddening as they are, these lists are crucial. If I forget to send a card to my editor's assistant, then my next check mysteriously disappears for three weeks. If I innocently omit the reviewer who gave my latest book such a rave, then the phrase "a piece of trash" is sure to appear in her critique of my next one. And when friends are forgotten in the madness? Let's just say that weeping is involved.

Once the final lists are drawn up, the tension shifts to choosing the perfect card. The holiday card must be something personal, a reflection of me. No longer can I get away with sending the same thing everyone else is sending. Now I have to pick something clever. The worst shame any queen can endure is to find out that the card he thought was so unique, so witty, so absolutely fabulous, has been sent out by three other queens who just happened to go to the same store.

Have you ever tried to find something completely and utterly "you" while looking at stacks of cards that come ten to a package for $15, calculating that you need at least 13 boxes, and trying not to throw up? It's not easy, I can tell you. Of *course* I want to be a daring individual. Of *course* I want to send those hand-painted vellum cards from Italy that require extra postage because of the need for hand canceling. But the thought of paying $4 for each of those little pieces of art makes that box of 75 cards with pictures of kittens wearing Santa hats that's on sale for $6 at Wal-Mart look pretty appealing.

And it's not just the outside I have to worry about. I also have to consider the message within. Not everyone appreciates a jolly "Merry Christmas" greeting. I need to worry about my Jewish friends. And my pagan friends. And my American Indian friends. And everyone else out there who isn't into the whole ho-ho-ho thing. I used to have one pile of yule cards, one pile of Hanukkah cards, one pile of "season's greetings" cards, and a pile of generic, snowy-looking cards. But then I would get all confused and send my Jewish editor a Kwanza card, and my pagan friends were not really all that pleased to see baby Jesus when they opened their envelopes. To avoid such problems, I now demand one-size-fits-all. And let me tell you, that's not easy to find.

Let's assume, for the sake of argument, that this is a perfect world and I manage both to find cards that work for everyone and the bank gives me a loan to purchase them. The battle still isn't over. Now I have to write something in them. *All* of them. The printed greeting is not enough. Nor is a simple signature. That looks cheap and unfeeling. At least that's what my publicist told me last year when I tried it on his card.

No, everyone wants a personal message, something to convince them that I have a reason for remembering them after not having spoken to them all year. This means I actually have to think of a good reason for sending each card. Sometimes that's easy. I usually remember why I like my friends, or at least I know what they want to believe I like about them. And telling your agent that she "makes life worth living" is always sure to bring a smile. But occasionally a name pops up on the list that I can't for the life of me put a face to. Clearly there was a reason for adding the person to the roster back in July, but what was it?

In those cases, I have to come up with something vague yet cheerful. "Wishing you the best in this joyous season" is always nice. Even if the recipient isn't into Christmas or Hanukkah or whatever, it's always winter, and there's no reason not to be happy about it. But even then you never know. Last year I found a dozen names on my list that, despite days of racking my brain, I couldn't account for. Undaunted, I wrote out cards to them all with the message "May the new year be as good to you as this one has been" and sent them off with a feeling of satisfaction.

A week later, the phone calls started coming in.

"Um, hi," said the first caller. "I just wanted to say I think your card was in really poor taste given what happened between us."

As it turned out, I'd gotten my lists mixed up. The unfamiliar names had come from a list of writers whose work I'd soundly rejected for an anthology I'd put together earlier in the year. The list I'd meant to use contained the names of editors who had expressed interest in seeing the manuscript for my new novel. I hurriedly dashed off cards to them all, but it was too late. The card season had passed. When I sent my manuscript out a few months later, none of them responded.

Even after the cards are bought, written, and sent out, I still can't relax. Every year, about ten days after I send out my cards, I start getting cards in return. But I don't enjoy it, because I'm not convinced those people actually meant to send me cards. I think they only did it because they got mine and felt obligated. This simply adds to my agony. I hate to think that I'm not already on someone's list and that I only get cards from them out of guilt.

So I keep track of the days that go by between the time I send my cards out and when I start getting them from others. Three or four days in between suggests that our cards crossed in the mail, bringing a sigh of relief. Anything beyond that and I get suspicious. Then I have to examine the received card minutely for clues. One with a scribbled signature and no message is suspect, but if the card is appealing enough, I let it slide. One that looks like it came from a sampler pack, or that has a pre-printed address label, however, is a bad one, and I remove the sender from my own list.

I know, I sound petty and awful. I'm still better than my friend Francesca. She actually keeps a list on her refrigerator of all her friends' names. If one of us fails to send her an appropriate card, she doesn't say anything. She just crosses the unlucky person's name off with heavy black marker. Then, when we go to her house for her annual holiday party, our shame is right there for everyone to see every time they open the freezer for more ice. It's a fate worse than death. You can imagine the wonderful cards she gets. I enclose cash in mine.

So here I am again. I've made my lists. I've checked them twice. I'm sitting here surrounded by mountains of cards. I'm working feverishly to get them all written and mailed in time. That said, I would like to take this opportunity to say that if you don't receive one, it's not because I don't like you. It's just that my hand cramped up.

Do You Have Any That Are Already Trained?

Everyone is getting babies. I mean everyone. And when I say getting, I mean acquiring. Because nowadays there are options. Some of them are actually having these babies the old-fashioned way. Mostly the lesbians. They've armed themselves with ovulation charts and turkey basters and empty baby food jars for their male friends to fill with sperm. But the boys are in on it too, busily finding female friends who want to go "halfsies" on an infant. I even have an FTM friend who kept his vagina in case he ever wanted to do the motherhood thing. Now he's eight months pregnant, and with his beard and hairy chest everyone just assumes he's a bear. It's a brave new world, folks, and we queers are leading the way.

The ones who aren't making their babies from scratch are even more determined. Some of them are adopting, wading through expensive miles of red tape and coming out the other side parents. Others, the ones with bad credit or blots on their records that prevent them from adopting, are apparently finding babies at tag sales, because they're all getting them one way or another. Every time I turn around, another of my friends is waving a baby picture in my face and telling me about the latest addition to the family.

"Sorry I haven't called you in three weeks," said my friend Craig when he finally phoned after I'd left a string of increasingly worried messages. "I was in Cambodia picking up Matt."

"I thought you were dating some waiter named John," I said.

Craig chuckled in an oddly paternal way. "No, Matt is my new son. I adopted him from an orphanage there. I did a lot of research and found that it's easier than adopting in the States."

Craig is a man who once put a cat to sleep for using the new issue of *Vanity Fair* as a scratching post. His condo is a museum for all things expensive and breakable. He has white wall-to-wall carpeting. Him with a child is like Jesse Helms with a soul. The two just don't go together.

"What are you going to do with a baby?" I asked, curious.

"It's really great," he said with a contented sigh. "I feel like my life is complete now."

This is the same thing Craig said when he found a pair of Kenneth Cole dress shoes at half-off, *and* when he located the last place setting of his discontinued china pattern, *and* when he had liposuction to remove the final seven pounds that prevented him from wearing a Speedo in public.

But the really scary thing is that Craig is far from alone. It used to be that one of the advantages of being a gay man was you didn't have to spend great amounts of time and money raising children. A lot of us thought this was a great fringe benefit. No kids meant more money for things like traveling to Italy, seeing Broadway shows, and purchasing a new wardrobe every season. It also meant not having to hire baby-sitters when we went clubbing until 3 in the morning, and being able to have sex in the living room whenever we wanted to without fear of interruption.

Not anymore. Now, instead of aspiring to be daddies, a lot of gay men apparently want to be *daddies*. My friend Susie travels all over the country giving lectures to college students about sexuality. Mostly her audiences are filled with queer kids, since the straight ones are afraid she's going to ask them to get in touch with their anuses or something. A while back Susie started asking her audiences if any of them planned on having children. She thought maybe a few would say yes. To her surprise, she finds that wherever she goes almost every gay man in the group raises his hand. "It's the straight girls and the gay boys," she says, mystified. "They all want to be mommies."

Far be it from me to be pessimistic, but I can't help being the tiniest bit suspicious about this whole baby thing, especially when all the gay men I know are suddenly popping up with toddlers in tow. These are the same people who rushed out to buy dalmatian puppies a few years ago when Disney released that awful live-action movie about the spotted canines. Now the animal shelters are brimming with yelping three-year-old dogs because the poor things had the nerve to shed copiously on their owners' black sweaters and sully the pristine expanse of the leather sofa. I don't want to think about what will happen when all these newfound human kids start coloring on the walls and leaving spit-up on daddy's $235 Hugo Boss tie.

I'm not saying that gay men don't make great fathers.

I know lots of fantastic gay men who have raised or are raising children. I just find it disconcerting that it's happening so suddenly and in such large numbers. It's the new gay obsession, kind of like when queer boys everywhere simultaneously started wearing Calvin Klein boxer briefs. Now, instead of sporting the same underwear or hairstyle, gay men recognize each other on the street by the fact that they are all walking along pushing similarly outfitted strollers.

"Where did you get yours?" has become the new pickup line as men coo and smile at one another's babies.

"China," comes the answer. "I went there because there was a better selection. In Russia you get what they bring you."

"I made mine myself," another proud father might say as he adjusts his child's Baby Gap overalls, "with a little help from a lesbian friend and the October issue of *Honcho*."

This is all well and good while the children are young and cute. But, like puppies, babies grow into gangly children with bad attitudes and nasty habits. What happens then? Sure, that bundle of joy looks adorable all dressed up in a smart outfit from Donna Karan Jr., but what about when she announces that she wants to wear ripped jeans and a polyester tube top? Even worse, suppose she shows a penchant for corduroy and sandals with socks? By that point it's too late, and gay nerves everywhere will be shot beyond repair.

Not to mention adolescence and the whole sex thing. If it's true that your parents don't make you gay, then we have to assume that the majority of children born to or raised by queer parents will grow up to be straight. Are we ready for that kind of disappointment? Will we be supportive when they sit us down and say, "Dad. Dad. I have something to tell you." It's important to think about these things before you get excited over becoming a parent. After all, the thrill of planning a wedding only lasts until the ice sculpture swan dissolves into a warm puddle and the bills begin to arrive.

This risk of disappointment, I think, is why I have never wanted children. Or, I suppose it would be more accurate to say, it's why if I were to have a child I would want only a particular kind. A girl. With a bad attitude and a sharp mind—a mix of Fran Lebowitz, Janeane Garofalo, and Mary Matalin (but without the Republican leanings). I wouldn't be happy with anything else. Frankly, I don't believe those people who tell you that you love your children no matter how they come out. I would be so pissed off if my baby grew up to be stupid, or uninteresting, or David Hasselhoff. It would ruin the entire experience for me. So why take the risk?

Ultimately I'm afraid this baby thing is just a fad, like Freedom Rings and Billy dolls. So maybe we should treat it as one. If someone were smart, they'd start selling shares in babies like they do in houses on Fire Island and Key West. That way gay men could experience the thrill of fatherhood without the pesky commitment that usually goes along with it. For a few thousand dollars, you could get two weeks with little Mei-Lin or baby Torsten, delivered right to your door with all of the necessary accoutrements. Several friends could even go in together, making it more affordable. At the end of the share, those interested in going all the way could make arrangements for more permanent situations, and those who found child rearing too demanding would return to their lives with no regrets. Even better, the next year they could order a totally different kid, thereby always remaining on the cutting edge of parenthood and avoiding the stigma of being seen walking the same child twice.

As I say, I'm all for having options, and I'm pleased that so many queers are realizing they can do the kiddie thing if they so choose. There's no reason anyone should be deprived of the satisfaction of saying "I told you so" to a 13-year-old who has just found out the hard way that daddy wasn't kidding when he said Ecstasy and beer don't mix. I, however, will stick to having a dog. It's much easier to maintain control over someone entirely motivated by food, and since he probably won't live past the age of 12, I never have to worry about him wanting to borrow the car.

The Condensed History of Queer Sex

Sex and gay men have always gone hand in hand, or, in some parts of our community, hand in ass. Like it or not (and most of us *do* like it), we are always going to be identified and defined, at least in part, by our sexuality. It is an integral part of who we are as gay men, and often it is a reflection of larger events in our lives. Just as we've seen enormous changes in other areas, so too has the expression of our sexuality changed depending upon the social, political, and even artistic climate of the times. Some of these changes have been good ones; others have been a drag. But through it all, we have managed to enthusiastically maintain our ability to enjoy a good fuck. In celebration of our sexual past, I offer these highlights from our most sacred of histories.

The Seventh Day: While God, weary from six days of nonstop creation, is resting, two of his creations, Adam and Steve, spend a long afternoon exploring the many pleasures of their newly formed bodies. Suffering from jealousy, one of the less endowed angels wakes God and tells him a nasty lie about Steve and a snake, thus establishing himself as both the first closet case and the first fundamentalist. As punishment, Steve's name and penis are both severely shortened, forever altering history.

1543 B.C.: Hearing that things are better in big cities, gay men flock to the metropolises of Sodom and Gomorrah. Things go well until some Christians show up and start trouble with a group of drunken straight men. As usual, everything is blamed on the queers, and God, still pissed over the whole Adam-and-Steve thing, acts before hearing both sides of the story.

858 B.C.: After a long period of decline, man-on-man sex is repopularized by Faggotus, a Greek party promoter looking for a way to enliven the declining nightlife industry in Athens. His new club, MIVM, is an immediate success, and homosexuality quickly spreads throughout the empire. Because the Greeks don't believe in the Christian God anyway, that whole mess is averted.

328 A.D.: While sex between men is officially forbidden as a remnant of non-Christian societies, many converts have difficulty keeping their desires in check. Thankfully, the Catholic Church is invented, providing gay men with a haven where they can express their true selves while avoiding persecution. The priesthood is established. Monasteries are formed. The arts flourish.

1509: Michelangelo, deciding it is high time for a gay porn magazine, is thwarted when he finds it difficult to mass produce nude images on paper. Instead, he paints the pictures directly onto the ceiling of the Sistine Chapel, where they are admired by many.

1874: William Chambers, a farm hand in North Carolina, places what is believed to be the first gay personal ad when the following appears in *Crooked Furrows*, an agricultural journal: "Comely fellow with bountiful seed seeking man with sturdy equipment to plow his field. No fats or femmes."

1954: With the gay community still largely underground, the now-familiar "One-Two-Three-Turn" technique of street cruising is introduced as a way of identifying potential partners. Across the country, men develop whiplash after cruising their own reflections while passing department store windows.

1969: The Summer of Love takes on new meaning when the Stonewall riots put gay issues front and center. Suddenly queer sex becomes a political statement, and men everywhere are filled with the spirit of liberation. Unfortunately, this often requires treatment with large doses of penicillin afterward.

1973: The American Psychiatric Association declares that engaging in homosexual acts will no longer be considered a sign of mental illness. Initially, 48% of its voting membership disagree until the other 52% threaten to publish compromising photos of the dissenters taken at the annual Christmas party.

1976: The Glory (Hole) Days. Fueled by the intoxicating combination of disco, mustache wax, and polyester fibers, gay men launch a sexual free-for-all, complete with costumes and dance numbers. For a while, the greatest problem facing queer boys is how to get those unsightly Crisco stains out of cotton sheets.

1981: The first cases of what is initially called "gay cancer" are reported in New York City, and are quickly linked to sexual activities. Shortly thereafter, angry politicians call for bathhouses around the country to be shut down because, in their opinion, people are unable able to make choices about their health for themselves.

1983: As the AIDS epidemic grows, phone sex offers a safe alternative to the real thing. The number of available lines proliferates, and confusion results when fervent Christians trying to reach the recently disconnected 1-900-GODTALK instead reach 1-900-GOFUCKK and don't know whether to press 1 for tops or 2 for bottoms.

1986: When police enter a Georgia man's home on an unrelated matter and find him engaged in sex with another man, he is charged under the state's antiquated sodomy law. The case, *Bowers v. Hardwick*, goes to the Supreme Court, where in a 5–4 ruling, the Court declares that the idea of two men doing it is really icky, even if the people involved have no problem with it whatsoever.

1990: Determined to prove once and for all that Safe Sex=Hot Sex, two ACT UP demonstrators attempt to achieve simultaneous orgasms while totally encased in plastic wrap and seated at opposite ends of a room. Their theory is shaken when, instead of coming, they spontaneously combust.

1994: Online chat rooms and sex-related Web sites quickly replace bars as the meeting place of choice for gay men. Curiously, it is discovered that 98% of gay men are 6' 2" with swimmers' builds and eight-inch cocks.

1999: A number of young gay men, totally pissed off over not having been old enough in the 1970s to have sex, launch the barebacking movement in an attempt to recreate what they consider the true spirit of the times. Shortly thereafter, angry gay activists call for bathhouses around the country to be shut down because, in their opinion, people are unable able to make choices about their health for themselves.

Along Came a Spider

I locked myself out of the house today.

Normally I wouldn't do such a thing. I'm fairly compulsive about always having my keys with me when I go out the front door, which locks automatically. I've forgotten on a couple of occasions and learned my lesson, and it hasn't happened in a very long time. But today there were extenuating circumstances. Namely, the spider.

I'd been spending a lovely morning lying on the bed watching the French Open, where Monica Seles was kicking Conchita Martinez's butt in the quarterfinals. I didn't have anything else to do all day, and I was extremely pleased about it. It was especially nice to see Monica doing so well again. Then, as Monica prepared to serve for the match, I rolled over and looked at the ceiling. There, clinging to the edge of the light fixture, was the spider.

I don't like spiders. Not in the least. They have too many legs and too many eyes. I don't care if they eat pests and make pretty webs. I have hated them since childhood, when a very large one fell on my head. I even hated Charlotte in *Charlotte's Web*. I wanted someone to step on her.

This spider was definitely looking at me and waiting for the right moment to drop. I know that if I hadn't spotted it first, it would have had all eight of its creepy little spider legs in my hair in an instant. To make matters worse, I was wearing only boxer shorts. I'm sure to the spider all that bare skin looked like an all-you-can-eat buffet.

As it was, we had a face-off. I lay there beneath the light, my eyes glued to the shifty arachnid hovering above me, afraid that any movement at all on my part would create air currents and cause it to tumble off the light and onto my naked self. So there I stayed for about ten minutes, watching for signs of attack and trying not to breathe too heavily.

Finally, when I thought the spider was occupied with something else, I flung myself sideways off the bed and onto the floor with a crash. I could hear the spider hissing with irritation as I scrambled for safety, but it stayed where it was. I kept one eye on it as I slipped into the hallway and grabbed the broom from the closet; I didn't want it to get away, which would have then required an entire day of ripping the room apart and looking for it just to make sure it wasn't lurking in the sheets.

Despite being armed with the broom, I was at a disadvantage. The spider was near the ceiling, and there was a chance it would fall on me when whacked. Or, worse, it might fall on the bed and pretend to be dead until I tried to pick it up, when it would suddenly spring to life and lunge at my throat. Thinking quickly, I flicked the light on and off a few times, hoping the strobe effect would momentarily blind the nasty critter, or that maybe some stray electricity would zap it for me.

Then, channeling Xena, I went for it. Pushing the broom at the spider, I tried to put a swift end to things. But he wasn't giving in easily, and instead of curling up in a little lifeless spider ball, he crawled onto the broom and made right for me, every facet of every compound eye glinting madly.

I figured I had about ten seconds to get down the hall and out the front door before the spider managed to skitter up the length of the handle and onto my arm. So you can see how I might have forgotten the little matter of the keys. It was hard enough to run and scream at the same time.

But I did it, and soon I was on the porch, vigorously beating the broom over the railing and waiting for the spider to tumble off. Which it did. Right into the garden. That's fine. I don't mind spiders in the garden. As long as they stay there. I just don't like it when they put all their spidery horribleness in my face.

Yes, I know. I'm about 39 billion times bigger than a spider. And I know all those egghead scientists *say* spiders aren't generally poisonous. That's small comfort. The little buggers are sneaky. Give them half a chance and they'll dart up your pants and disappear. At that point, all the dancing around and smacking at yourself you can manage won't fix things. I've tried that.

My friends think my spider paranoia is amusing, especially because I don't mind any other bug, snake, or generally nasty thing. But my friends don't know what it's like to be cornered in a wood shed with a spider hanging in the only exit. And I sincerely doubt that any of them has ever been stuck in a small tent at night and seen the outline of a descending spider silhouetted against the canopy. I don't think they would think spiders were so much fun after that.

They *would*, however, all think it was very funny to see me—a grown man—on the porch in my boxer shorts beating at the door and yelling for the dog to let me in. I'm sure they would also get a big chuckle out of seeing me run madly through the backyard before the spider could crawl back up on the porch for round two. And I'm sure they would find it amusing beyond words to know I had to break into my own bedroom window to get safely back inside.

Go ahead, call me a sissy. I don't care. And when you wake up one day mummified in spider silk, don't come crying to me. I'll be hiding under the bed.

If the Shoe Fits

I recently read that Milton Berle is suing a gay news-paper because one of its advertisers used a photograph of him in drag. At first I assumed he was suing because they had used his likeness without paying for it. But no. He says the ad implies he's gay, and he's suing for defamation of character.

First of all, who even knew Milton Berle was still alive? If he is—and I have my doubts—he must be about 600 years old. Secondly, the last time I saw him on television his face looked like a gigantic, bloated scrotum. Hardly the stuff of erotic fantasies, even if all those rumors about the his ample endowment are true.

This is why I don't see what he's all agitated about. It's not as if gay men, misreading the ad, are going to send him mash notes and their panties. And it isn't as if he's going to lose out on any choice acting roles because of this. After all, the man walked around in a dress for much of his career and it didn't hurt him one bit. Maybe the *Touched by an Angel* people will think twice about casting him as a dying senator who needs to reunite with his ex-prostitute daughter, but that hardly seems worth a lawsuit.

I think he's just still pissed off about the time he had to appear on the MTV Music Video Awards with RuPaul and Ru read him but good for being the obnoxious bore that he is. Upstaged by a queer, he had to fight back, and this was the only thing he could think of. And what was Uncle Miltie doing reading a gay newspaper in the first place?

This whole "who is" and "who isn't" celebrity thing is getting tired anyway. Didn't we learn our lesson with Jodie Foster and Richard Gere? Apparently not, since the tabloids and even the mainstream media are constantly speculating about who's putting what in whose whatever. Remember all that speculation about Whitney Houston and her gal pal? Now Janet Jackson is in the spotlight after holding hands with some girl at an awards show. But Janet, unlike Whitney, is smart enough to not make a big deal about it, and is letting people think whatever they want to think. Good for her.

Then there's Simon Rex. He's that former MTV "personality" turned television actor who once made a gay porn video. All he did in it was jerk off by himself, something he probably still does a couple of times a week. But because it was caught on tape and sold to a gay audience, everyone got all excited and talked about how it was going to ruin his career. The idea that someone who introduces videos made by musicians who shoot themselves full of heroin and routinely get arrested for all kinds of felonies might find his job in jeopardy because he played with himself once on film is a little unbelievable to me, especially considering the antics of Tommy and Pamela Anderson Lee. But Rex, who left MTV to pursue other options, is now all over the place proclaiming his heterosexuality and saying the video was the biggest mistake of his life.

Being obsessed with sex is nothing new in our culture, so it's not surprising that people like to speculate about whether someone is gay. I confess that even I have, on occasion, checked to see if some hunky actor who has caught my eye is married, especially if he's played gay on television or in a movie. What I don't get, though, is why stars still think being gay—or being perceived as gay—is the worst thing anyone could possibly say about them. They'll go on television and talk freely about their eating disorders or their debilitating drug use, but suggest that they might be homos and they'll start a publicity campaign to prove otherwise. When country stud Ty Herndon was arrested in a men's room for soliciting an undercover cop, he actually thought it would be better for his reputation to say he was offering sex only in exchange for drugs, as if deep-throating a cop is fine as long as you get some uppers for it.

If you look at the handful of celebrities who have come out, most of them are doing pretty well. Rupert Everett has more movie offers than he can handle. Ian McKellen won praise and an Oscar nomination for his work in *Gods and Monsters*. Even Ellen keeps showing up in films. Yet stars still cower in the closet, terrified to open the door even a crack. Kevin Spacey, for instance, is a wonderful actor, but when he tells *Playboy* he welcomes rumors of his homosexuality because it makes him even more popular with the ladies, I want to smack him. And when an amazing comic talent like Sean Hayes of *Will & Grace* suddenly starts avoiding questions he answered openly before his rise to fame, I have to wonder what everyone is so afraid of.

And they *are* afraid. That's why we have ridiculous situations like Milton Berle suing a gay newspaper that probably doesn't have enough money to meet its printing costs, let alone settle a lawsuit filed by some wealthy has-been with nothing better to do. It's why the lesbian magazine *Deneuve* had to become *Curve*. (Pouty French actress Catherine Deneuve assumed they were both implying something about her sexuality and trying to trade on her name. As if anyone anywhere cares who she's bedding.) It's why Tom and Nicole took out a full-page newspaper ad informing the world they aren't queer and are tired of people thinking they are. Not that it did any good.

Not that *any* of their denials do any good. How many people really think Whitney Houston loves Bobby Brown, no matter how many times she bails him out of jail? Probably the same number who insisted George Michael was straight before his arrest and coming out. How many people are actually stupid enough to think Rosie O'Donnell can't possibly be a muff diver because she babbles on about Tom Cruise? And speaking of Tom, how many people do you know who swear they have a friend who blew him at a party in Key West, or know a guy who slept with Ricky Martin before he made it big? Maybe it's true and maybe it's not. The point is, we love this stuff, and no matter what the stars say it isn't going to disappear. So the gay ones might as well fess up and let us be proud of our own.

My straight friends like to ask me who's gay and who isn't. I don't know why they think I have the inside scoop, but they do. They think every gay person knows all the other gay people, like we have a directory or something. But the truth is, even I am usually surprised when someone famous admits his homosexuality. I'm so used to everyone denying it that I don't really believe anyone is until I have hard proof, so to speak. Even then I'm not always convinced it isn't a publicity stunt. Remember David Bowie's bisexuality?

Not everyone is so uptight, thankfully, and I'm happy about that. A few years back a rugby team in New Zealand made their players' already short shorts even shorter because they knew gay fans liked to look at the men's butts and crotches. That's when I knew that there really is a God, and that he's queer too. More recently, a couple of Brazilian soccer players posed nude for a gay magazine there, even though they aren't gay. They told reporters that they just thought it would be fun. Good for them. And when that cute fellow in the pop group Boyzone came out, their web site and management offices were jammed with e-mails and letters from 13-year-old girls offering their support and saying how brave he was. If a teen idol can say he's a cocksucker and become even more popular, I think that says something about what fans are willing to accept. So how come so few stars listen to them?

I just wish more stars would relax about the whole gay thing, whether they're gay or not. When I titled one of my books *Alec Baldwin Doesn't Love Me*, some people feared I would end up in a lawsuit. Instead, I received a lovely letter from Alec saying how much he enjoyed the book. I would have appreciated a pair of his boxer shorts, but it was still sporting of him. He didn't even hold it against me when the *New York Post* ran excerpts from the book in an effort to embarrass him. I wish more stars would take the same approach. But until they do, I guess I shouldn't title my next book *Milton Berle Is a Big Old Knob Gobbler*.

Why I Am Queer

A while ago I received a letter from a reader, a gay man, who said he objected to my use of the word *queer* to describe myself and other lesbian and gay people. He said he believed that it sets gay people apart as something strange and out of the norm, and hearing it applied to himself made him feel alienated. "I love what you have to say," he wrote, "but I wish you would stop using that word."

I understand his feelings, but I like *queer*. I like it precisely *because* it means "strange and unusual," and also because it implies that the person being referred to in some way causes others to be just the tiniest bit nervous. Things that are queer make people question their perceptions and reevaluate what their definitions of things are. Come across something queer and your worldview is altered, if only for a moment.

Words and what they mean is an obsession of mine. I suppose it's an occupational hazard. I especially like seeing how the meanings of words can change over time. I spend a fair amount of time in used-book stores, and a number of years ago I started noticing the word *queer* in the titles of many books. Mostly they were books from the early 1900s. At that time, *queer* meant something delightfully out of the ordinary, and the use of the word in the title of a book was a sure sign that the contents were going to be fun. In *Dorothy Dale's Queer Holidays*, for example, the heroine has all kinds of adventures that make her friends green with envy.

I love the idea of queer as something to be envied, something that not everyone can have or be. One of the nicest things a straight friend ever said to me was, "I wish I could be queer. It seems like such fun." She's right. It is fun. It's fun to show the world that there are other ways to live besides the ones they're used to seeing. It's fun to escape the boundaries of cut-and-dried roles like "straight" and "gay," with all their accompanying baggage. It's fun to define for yourself who and what you are.

But somewhere along the line, *queer* apparently stopped being fun. It hardly ever appears in book titles after about 1940. I don't know why. I like to imagine there was some great defining moment, some scandalous event that caused everyone to stop using *queer* because instead of indicating daring and adventure it instead implied notoriety. Like maybe there was an infamous New York City gangster family who called themselves the Queens Queers and who were known for their particularly stylish ways of knocking off enemies. Probably, though, it was simply a matter of language changing with time.

Whatever the reason, *queer* was out for a long time. Then, in the early 1980s, Elizabeth Levy wrote *Something Queer is Going On*, the first in a series of more than a dozen "Something Queer" books for children. Once again, *queer* was fun. Her heroines had all kinds of, well, queer adventures. They had queer adventures in the library and in the Wild West. They found queer clues and solved queer mysteries. They were funny and smart, and kids loved them because of their queerness.

Coincidentally, around the same time Levy's books appeared, Queer Nation chapters sprang up in cities like New York and San Francisco. *Queer* was back with a vengeance. But it didn't come back without opposition. Some people—a lot of people—hated it. They said it was ill-mannered and impudent. They said it reeked of self-loathing. They tried to stick it back in the box with *neato* and *groovy*. But *queer* was stronger than that. It stuck around, and gradually more and more same-sex folks tried it on for size and found that it fit just fine.

Now queer has become the flavor of the month for people outside the gay world. I have another straight friend, a man, who likes to say about himself, "I'm not gay, but I'm queer." What he means is that while his own sex life is garden-variety heterosexual, he appreciates and supports other sexual activities and ways of being. In other words, he likes to look at lesbian porn and sometimes he lets his wife spank him.

While I agree that this man is more interesting than most of the straight men I know, I have to disagree with his assessment of himself as queer. Being queer is about much more than supporting other people in their difference; it is about *being* different in ways that make it impossible for you to fit the norm. Straight people can be different. They can be unusual. They can even be complete freaks. But as long as they're straight, they're going to have it easier than people who aren't. They aren't going to be queer.

In this time when many gay activists and public figures are calling for homos to be like everyone else, queer is a dangerous thing to be. Assimilation and blending in offer comfort to some and protection to others. I can understand this. For many of us, especially those of us who have experienced discrimination or worse because of our sexuality, the idea of fitting in, or even just being left alone, can be very appealing.

But for others, blending in means the death of the spirit. A friend of mine who grew up and still lives in the middle of the Bible Belt said the other day, "Being just like everyone else is a luxury in big cities. People there have the option of fitting in or not. But for those of us in the rest of America, fitting in is a requirement. We do it because it's the only way we can survive. So when someone tells me that the best way for the gay community to get ahead is to be as much like straight people as possible, it makes me furious. I would love to be able to be queer, to be out and visible and outrageous if I want to be. But I can't. I don't have that option. To me, being just like everyone else is to be invisible and imprisoned."

I've never fit in very well. I don't fit into the straight world, and I don't fit neatly into the gay world. Growing up, I had the word *queer* scrawled on my locker at school and spat at me by boys in gym class when I screwed up. Their hate made me sad, but the word never did. I knew I wasn't like them, and that I didn't want to be like them, even if it meant never being hated. I was queer then, and I still am. I am queer because I love men in a world that still thinks that isn't the way to go. I am queer because I refuse to believe there is only one way to be. I am queer because I choose to be, and because it's who and what I am.

Once upon a time, it was fine to be gay. We needed to band together under a common name. But gay doesn't cut it in the long run. For one thing, it leaves out women. I know, women can be gay too. But if *gay* was meant to be inclusive of everyone, we wouldn't also have the word *lesbian*, would we? There is a logic to language, even if the people who think *he* and *man* should be assumed to include everyone don't agree.

I know *gay* is a convenient shorthand, and I use it myself when other terms might be more comprehensive but also more cumbersome. But I wonder how many men would be happy if, instead of *gay*, we decided *lesbian* was all-encompassing? I remember once writing a paper for a class in college and using the word *she* where I would normally have used the generic *he*. I got it back with a note from the (male) professor saying, "This is very distracting. Why change from the standard?"

Maybe because sometimes the standards don't work anymore, or never did in the first place, unless you happened to belong to the group whose designation was chosen to mean everyone, however inappropriately. I don't mind being gay. I really don't. But I don't know why that word was chosen. Was there some kind of committee? Because it seems a little random to me. At least *lesbian* makes sense: women who lived on Lesbos and were thought to have had sexual and romantic relationships with one another. What's *gay*? Light and frivolous. Happy and carefree.

Frankly, I suspect *gay* was originally applied to homosexuals in the same condescending way *queer* was. We were seen as something whimsical, perhaps even transitory or ephemeral, and not to be taken seriously. Maybe we chose it for ourselves. I don't know. I wasn't there. But however it came about, we took it on and made it our own.

Many of us are doing the same with *queer*. And, personally, I think *queer* is a much better word than *gay*. It has a sense of defiance, whereas *gay* feels slightly defeatist. It has a tired resignation to it, like the funny old bachelor uncle you have who always wears a cardigan and bedroom slippers and who raises orchids. *Queer* is more of an upstart, the girl in leather pants who rides her motorcycle through a crowd of catcalling men and gives them the finger as she passes by.

Ultimately, I think the division over the word *queer* is a sign that the community is maturing. We have never been a homogenous community. We are just a group of people with a common link. Apart from that link, we are all very different. The fact that we no longer accept the lie that one word fits all is a tribute to our growing independence. It may make some of us nervous because it threatens to shatter the illusion of oneness we've perpetuated for far too long, but sooner or later all movements need to outgrow themselves.

So be *gay*. Be *queer*. Be *homosexual*. Be a faggot or a pansy or a fairy, a dyke or a bulldagger or a butch. Be anything you want to be. Fit in or stand out or live somewhere in between. But whatever you decide to be, be it with as much joy and strength as you possibly can. Because ultimately it doesn't matter what we put on our banners and signs. What matters is being who we are, and not what someone else wants us to be.

About the Author

Michael Thomas Ford's previous essay collections, *Alec Baldwin Doesn't Love Me* and *That's Mr. Faggot to You*, remained on best-seller lists for months, earning him unanimous critical praise and back-to-back Lambda Literary Awards for humor. In addition to his books he writes a syndicated monthly newspaper column, "My Queer Life," which runs in dozens of papers, and his weekly online radio show of the same name airs weekly on The Stellar Networks at www.gaybc.com. He has contributed fiction and essays to numerous anthologies and magazines, and he wrote the libretto for *Alec Baldwin Doesn't Love Me*, a musical based on his work. He is currently finishing up a novel, so stop asking. And if you want to know more about him, visit his Web site at www.michaelthomasford.com.